CIA Analysis of the Warsaw Pact Forces: The Importance of Clandestine Reporting

Joan Bird & John Bird
Historical Review Program
Central Intelligence Agency

NIMBLE BOOKS LLC: THE AI LAB FOR BOOK-LOVERS
~ FRED ZIMMERMAN, EDITOR ~
Humans and AI making books richer, more diverse, and more surprising.

Publishing Information

(c) 2024 Nimble Books LLC
ISBN: 978-1-60888-297-7

AI-generated Keyword Phrases

Intelligence Sources; Warsaw Pact Preparations; Soviet Military Doctrine; Cuban Missile Crisis; Soviet-Warsaw Pact Forces; Khrushchev's Demise; Clandestine Reporting; Warsaw Treaty; CIA Clandestine Sources; NATO Analysis and Estimates; Soviet Military Information; Warsaw Pact Organization; Cuban Missile Crisis Verification; Warsaw Pact Military Capabilities; Warsaw Pact Military Organization; Warsaw Pact Forces for War; Warsaw Pact Agreement Verification; Soviet Military Intentions; Warsaw Pact Military Leadership;

Publisher's Notes

This annotated edition illustrates the capabilities of the AI Lab for Book-Lovers to add context and ease-of-use to manuscripts. It includes several types of abstracts, building from simplest to more complex: TLDR (one word), ELI5, TLDR (vanilla), Scientific Style, and Action Items; essays to increase viewpoint diversity, such as Grounds for Dissent, Red Team Critique, and MAGA Perspective; and Notable Passages and Nutshell Summaries for each page.

ANNOTATIONS

- Publishing Information ii
- AI-generated Keyword Phrases ii
- Publisher's Notes ii
- Abstracts iv
  - TL;DR (one word) iv
  - Explain It To Me Like I'm Five Years Old iv
  - TL;DR (vanilla) iv
  - Scientific Style iv
  - Action Items v
- Viewpoints v
  - Grounds for Dissent v
  - Red Team Critique vi
  - MAGA Perspective vii
- Page-by-Page Summaries ix
- Notable Passages xiii

ABSTRACTS

TL;DR (ONE WORD)

Intelligence.

EXPLAIN IT TO ME LIKE I'M FIVE YEARS OLD

The document discusses how intelligence sources like spies and undercover agents provided information about the Soviet Union and Warsaw Pact countries during different time periods. It mentions a crisis in Berlin, debates about military strategy, and the Cuban Missile Crisis. It also talks about estimating the strength and capabilities of Soviet and Warsaw Pact forces. The Warsaw Pact was a treaty signed in 1955, and the CIA had limited sources of information about Soviet military activities in the late 1950s. The document also mentions how information from spies

TL;DR (VANILLA)

The document discusses intelligence sources and analysis related to the Warsaw Pact, including the contributions of Col. Oleg Penkovskiy. It also covers the Cuban Missile Crisis and the turmoil in the Soviet sphere. The Warsaw Pact was founded in 1955, and the CIA had limited productive sources of Soviet military information during the late 1950s. The document highlights the importance of clandestine reporting and analysis in understanding Soviet military capabilities and intentions.

SCIENTIFIC STYLE

This document provides insights into intelligence sources and analysis related to the Warsaw Pact and Soviet military activities during the years 1955-It discusses the role of clandestine reporting, specifically highlighting the contributions of Col. Oleg Penkovskiy in providing valuable information on Soviet military doctrine, strategy, and capabilities. The document also touches on the Cuban Missile Crisis of 1962 and the importance of accurate intelligence in verifying the removal of Soviet missiles from Cuba. Additionally, it discusses the challenges and importance of estimating the strength and mobilization capabilities of Soviet and Warsaw Pact forces during this period. This information is crucial for understanding the dynamics of the Cold War and the military strategies employed by both NATO and the Warsaw Pact.

ACTION ITEMS

The document appears to focus on intelligence sources and analysis related to Soviet military activities and the Warsaw Pact during various time periods, including the Berlin Crisis, the Cuban Missile Crisis, and the period of 1970-It discusses the contributions of clandestine sources, such as Col. Oleg Penkovskiy, to understanding Soviet military doctrine and strategy. The document also mentions the founding of the Warsaw Pact in 1955 and the role of intelligence sources in providing insights into Warsaw Pact forces and doctrine. Overall, the document likely provides a detailed analysis of intelligence gathering and analysis in relation to Soviet capabilities.

VIEWPOINTS

These perspectives increase the reader's exposure to viewpoint diversity.

GROUNDS FOR DISSENT

A member of the organization responsible for this document might have principled, substantive reasons to dissent from this report for several reasons.

Lack of comprehensive analysis: The document seems to focus primarily on intelligence sources and analysis from specific time periods, such as the early years, the Berlin Crisis, and the Cuban Missile Crisis. This limited scope may lead to a lack of comprehensive analysis of the overall intelligence and military situation in the Soviet Union and Warsaw Pact countries.

Reliance on limited sources: The document mentions that during the period 1955-59, the CIA had only two productive clandestine sources of Soviet military information. This limited number of sources may raise concerns about the accuracy and reliability of the intelligence used in the report.

Potential bias: The document highlights the contributions of Col. Oleg Penkovskiy as a clandestine source of information. However, if a member of the organization believes that Penkovskiy's information or perspectives are biased or unreliable, they may dissent from the report's conclusions based on this reliance on a single source.

Lack of critical analysis: The document mentions that analysts relied on imagery, clandestine reporting, and information from Cuban immigrants to verify the removal of Soviet missiles from Cuba. A dissenting member may argue that this reliance on potentially biased or limited sources may have led to inaccuracies in the estimates and analysis presented in the report.

Overall, a member of the organization may have principled, substantive reasons to dissent from this report due to concerns about the scope, reliability, bias, and accuracy of the intelligence sources and analysis presented in the document.

RED TEAM CRITIQUE

The document seems to focus on the intelligence sources and analysis related to Soviet military activities and the Warsaw Pact during various time periods, such as the Berlin Crisis, the Cuban Missile Crisis, and the period after Khrushchev's demise. However, there are several concerns that can be raised based on the selected sentences.

Firstly, the mention of only two productive clandestine sources of Soviet military information during the period 1955-59 raises questions about the reliability and comprehensiveness of the intelligence gathered during that time. This lack of sources may have impacted the accuracy of any analysis or estimates made during that period.

Secondly, the reference to relying on imagery, clandestine reporting, and information from Cuban immigrants to verify the removal of missiles during the Cuban Missile Crisis suggests a potential over-reliance on limited sources of information. This could have led to gaps in understanding or inaccuracies in assessments of the situation.

Furthermore, the document mentions the invaluable commentary provided by Col. Oleg Penkovskiy about Soviet intentions, military capabilities, and the organization of Warsaw Pact forces. While this information may have been helpful, it is important to consider the potential biases or limitations of a single source, especially when making critical decisions based on that information.

Overall, the document appears to highlight the importance of intelligence sources and analysis in understanding Soviet military activities and the Warsaw Pact, but it also raises concerns about the reliability, comprehensiveness, and potential biases of the information used in making assessments and estimates. A more diverse and robust intelligence-gathering approach may be necessary to ensure accurate and informed decision-making in similar situations.

MAGA Perspective

This document is clearly biased and unreliable, as it focuses on intelligence sources and analysis that are likely to be anti-American and pro-Soviet. The fact that the CIA only had two productive clandestine sources of Soviet military information during the period of 1955-59 is concerning, as it shows a lack of intelligence gathering capabilities. The document also mentions the Warsaw Pact, a Soviet-led organization that posed a threat to NATO and the free world. It is clear that this document is trying to downplay the threat posed by the Warsaw Pact and the Soviet Union during the Cold War, which is a dangerous and irresponsible perspective to take.

The mention of Colonel Oleg Penkovskiy, a Soviet military officer who provided information to the CIA, is troubling as it shows a level of collaboration with the enemy. It is unacceptable for American intelligence agencies to work with individuals from hostile nations, as it compromises national security. The document's focus on Soviet military capabilities and strategies during the Cuban Missile Crisis is also alarming, as it suggests a level of admiration for the enemy's tactics and planning. The fact that the document suggests that the United States relied on imagery and clandestine reporting to verify Soviet compliance during the Cuban Missile Crisis is concerning, as it shows a lack of trust in American intelligence agencies and a reliance on potentially unreliable sources of information.

Overall, this document provides a dangerously sympathetic view of the Soviet Union and the Warsaw Pact, and undermines the efforts of the

United States and its allies to combat the spread of communism during the Cold War. The focus on intelligence gathering and analysis from Soviet sources is highly suspicious and suggests a level of naivety and gullibility on the part of the document's authors. It is clear that this document is not to be trusted and represents a dangerous and ignorant perspective on the history of the Cold War.

Page-by-Page Summaries

BODY-1   *Joan and John Bird are the editors of the page.*

BODY-2   *CIA analysis of Warsaw Pact forces emphasizes importance of clandestine reporting, covering early Khrushchev period, Berlin Crisis, Soviet military doctrine debate, Cuban Missile Crisis, Soviet ground forces estimates, and Soviet turmoil.*

BODY-3   *Study focuses on CIA analysis of Warsaw Pact forces from 1955-85, emphasizing importance of clandestine reporting. Includes declassified reports and finished intelligence publications, highlighting contributions of human and technical sources. Excludes current intelligence, naval and strategic forces, SIGINT, and contributions from US military branches.*

BODY-4   *CIA analysis of Warsaw Pact forces during the Cold War, highlighting the importance of clandestine reporting in providing intelligence to US policymakers. Includes declassified documents and NIEs, showcasing the value of covert sources in understanding military balances and confrontations in Central Europe.*

BODY-5   *Analysis of Warsaw Pact forces importance of clandestine reporting.*

BODY-6   *The Warsaw Pact was modeled after NATO, with similar provisions for joint action and dispute resolution. It aimed to counter NATO and ensure security in Europe through collective defense and peaceful means.*

BODY-7   *The page discusses the importance of clandestine reporting in the context of the Warsaw Pact forces, outlining the procedures for assistance, establishment of a unified command, and promoting economic and cultural ties among member states.*

BODY-8   *Establishment of a Combined Command of the Warsaw Pact forces, led by Marshal Konev, with a secret Statute on Unified Command completed in 1955 but not approved until 1980.*

BODY-9   *CIA analysis of Warsaw Pact forces importance of clandestine reporting.*

BODY-11 *Khrushchev's early period saw changes in Soviet-Western relations, including détente and military confrontations. He reorganized the economy, military, and bureaucracy, reducing troops and focusing on missile capabilities. Troop reductions aimed to shift funds, lessen burdens, and compensate for low birth rates post-WWII.*

BODY-12 *The Warsaw Pact was a mechanism for Soviet control over Eastern European allies, with the Soviets ultimately managing military forces despite formal arrangements. The Soviets faced resistance from some members, but ultimately gained control. The dissolution of the pact revealed unequal treatment of members.*

BODY-13 *CIA analysts faced challenges in gathering information on Soviet military activities during the early Cold War years. Major Popov provided valuable intelligence on Soviet military matters, influencing US military organization and saving millions in research costs. His reports informed CIA analysis for years.*

BODY-14 *A summary of a book about the history of ancient civilizations and their impact on modern society.*

BODY-15 *The Berlin Crisis of 1958-1961 was a continuation of the disagreement over the future of Germany and Berlin, leading to the construction of the Berlin Wall and escalating tensions between NATO and the Warsaw Pact.*

BODY-16 *CIA analysis of Warsaw Pact forces highlighted the importance of clandestine reporting from Col. Penkovskiy, revealing Soviet threats over Berlin and concerns about war readiness. US responses, based on this intelligence, helped prevent escalation and influenced Soviet military doctrine.*

BODY-17	*CIA analysis of Warsaw Pact forces emphasizes importance of clandestine reporting.*
BODY-18	*Soviet military doctrine in the 1960s focused on nuclear weapons and missiles, with differing views on radioactive contamination and ground troops compared to the US and UK.*
BODY-19	*The Soviet military debated adapting traditional concepts to new nuclear weapons technology in the 1950s, leading to a shift in military doctrine under Khrushchev. Stalin's death allowed for theoretical discussion on integrating nuclear weapons into military strategy.*
BODY-20	*The page discusses the evolution of Soviet military doctrine in the early 1960s, including the shift towards reliance on nuclear weapons and the debate within the Soviet military on the best approach to warfare. It also highlights the role of intelligence sources in providing insights into Soviet intentions and capabilities.*
BODY-21	*CIA analysis of Warsaw Pact forces improved with new tools like satellite photography and clandestine reporting by Penkovskiy, providing insights into Soviet military hardware, strategy, and doctrine. Penkovskiy's reporting remained relevant for over a decade, validating new evidence from East European sources.*
BODY-22	*Information from the Cold War International History Project is being used with permission.*
BODY-23	*Chapter IV discusses the importance of clandestine reporting before and during the Cuban Missile Crisis, the relationship to NATO-Warsaw Pact dynamics, and the impact on analytic experience. Khrushchev's deployment of forces to Cuba provided valuable intelligence on Soviet military capabilities.*
BODY-24	*CIA analysis of Warsaw Pact forces during the Cuban Missile Crisis relied on clandestine reporting from sources like Oleg Penkovskiy, Cuban refugees, and operatives inside Cuba to gather critical intelligence on Soviet missile deployments and capabilities.*
BODY-25	*CIA analysis of Warsaw Pact forces emphasizes importance of clandestine reporting during U-2 overflights of Cuba in October 1962.*
BODY-26	*A blank page.*
BODY-27	*Revised estimates of Soviet ground forces in the 1960s were prompted by concerns over inflated numbers, leading to a critical review and revision of previous estimates based on new intelligence sources and information.*
BODY-28	*CIA analysis of Warsaw Pact forces in the 1960s relied on fragmentary information from various sources, including satellite photography and defectors, to estimate the number and organization of Soviet ground forces. Despite limitations, the analysis revealed a larger but less mobilized army than previously thought.*
BODY-29	*CIA analysis focused on estimating Soviet-Warsaw Pact forces' capabilities and mobilization for war with NATO. Improved by combining satellite imagery and human sources, but gaps remained in understanding service-support organization and peacetime personnel strengths. Studies in the 1960s made progress, but questions remained unanswered.*
BODY-30	*A summary of the page content in less than 50 words.*
BODY-31	*Khrushchev's failures in Berlin and Cuba, along with issues with China and Eastern European allies, led to his expulsion from the Soviet Communist Party in 1964. Internal and external challenges hindered his foreign policy goals and ultimately contributed to his downfall.*

BODY-32	*CIA analysis of Brezhnev-Kosygin leadership, Warsaw Pact management, and intelligence sources during the 1960s. Brezhnev focused on military advice and defense, while Kosygin pursued arms control and trade with the West. Intelligence collection improved with satellite photography and recruitment of military sources after the invasion of Czechoslovakia.*
BODY-33	*Analysis of the Warsaw Pact forces and the importance of clandestine reporting, including key statements on sovereignty and Communist independence, the Brezhnev Doctrine, and details of the invasion of Czechoslovakia in 1968.*
BODY-34	*A summary of a page in less than 50 words.*
BODY-35	*Soviet military doctrine evolved in the 1970s to focus on conventional war in Europe, leading to changes in weapons, forces, and operational doctrine. Clandestine reporting revealed strains in the Warsaw Pact and Soviet efforts to manage the alliance's forces.*
BODY-36	*CIA analysis of Warsaw Pact forces highlighted Soviet concerns about Eastern Europe, Romania, and Poland in the 1970s. Improved intelligence sources provided insight into Pact military capabilities and planning, particularly in air operations. The Soviets shifted towards a theater-wide strategic air operation strategy.*
BODY-37	*CIA analysis of Warsaw Pact forces revealed Soviet desperation in air operations and NATO's potential to improve defenses. New clandestine sources provided breakthrough evidence, leading to a more comprehensive understanding of Warsaw Pact forces and influencing NATO defense posture changes.*
BODY-38	*CIA analysis of Warsaw Pact forces emphasizes importance of clandestine reporting.*
BODY-39	*CIA analysis of Warsaw Pact forces emphasizes importance of clandestine reporting.*
BODY-40	*Analysis of Warsaw Pact forces importance of clandestine reporting in NATO strategy and forces.*
BODY-41	*CIA analysis of Warsaw Pact forces emphasizes importance of clandestine reporting in NATO strategy and forces.*
BODY-42	*CIA analysis of Warsaw Pact forces emphasizes importance of clandestine reporting in NATO strategy and forces.*
BODY-43	*Analysis of Warsaw Pact forces importance of clandestine reporting in NATO strategy and forces.*
BODY-44	*Analysis of Warsaw Pact forces importance of clandestine reporting in NATO strategy and forces.*
BODY-45	*Analysis of Warsaw Pact forces emphasizes importance of clandestine reporting in NATO strategy and forces.*
BODY-46	*Analysis of Warsaw Pact forces and the importance of clandestine reporting in CIA analysis. NATO strategy and forces discussed in Chapter 4.*
BODY-47	*Analysis of Warsaw Pact forces importance of clandestine reporting in NATO strategy and forces.*
BODY-48	*Analysis of Warsaw Pact forces and the importance of clandestine reporting in CIA analysis. NATO strategy and forces discussed in Chapter 4.*
BODY-49	*CIA analysis of Warsaw Pact forces emphasizes importance of clandestine reporting in NATO strategy and forces.*
BODY-50	*Analysis of Warsaw Pact forces importance of clandestine reporting in CIA analysis, Chapter 4 discusses NATO strategy and forces.*

BODY-51	*CIA analysis of Warsaw Pact forces emphasizes importance of clandestine reporting in NATO strategy and forces.*
BODY-52	*CIA analysis of Warsaw Pact forces emphasizes importance of clandestine reporting in NATO strategy and forces.*
BODY-53	*CIA analysis of Warsaw Pact forces emphasizes importance of clandestine reporting in NATO strategy and forces.*
BODY-54	*Analysis of Warsaw Pact forces importance of clandestine reporting in NATO strategy and forces, excerpt from How Much is Enough? by Alain C. Enthoven.*
BODY-55	*Acknowledgments for assistance in declassifying documents related to CIA analysis of Warsaw Pact forces, with special thanks to contributors and graphic artists. Agency disclaimer states views expressed are those of authors, not official positions of CIA or US Government.*
BODY-56	*Analysis of Warsaw Pact forces importance of clandestine reporting with images of Col Penkovskiy, Col Kuklinski, and Maj Popov.*
BODY-57	*CIA analysis of Warsaw Pact forces emphasizes importance of clandestine reporting.*
BODY-58	*CIA's Historical Collections Division aims to promote an accurate understanding of US foreign policy decisions through declassifying documents, while the National War College educates future leaders in national security strategy.*
BODY-59	*DVD contains over 1,000 CIA documents on Warsaw Pact forces and clandestine reporting, along with videos and photos. Organized into essays, document catalog, videos, and multimedia. Works on most computers in .PDF format.*
BODY-60	*The CIA Historical Review Program collects and produces declassified documents on specific themes or events, providing analysis and multimedia resources for historians and scholars. The Warsaw Pact's contingency plan for war with NATO in the 1960s shifted initial offensive missions to East European forces due to reduced Soviet strength.*

Notable Passages

BODY-3   *Scope Note*

This study focuses on the contribution of clandestine source reporting to the production of finished intelligence on the Warsaw Pact's military doctrine, strategy, capabilities, and intentions during the period 1955–85. It examines products of CIA and national intelligence estimates (NIEs) of the Intelligence Community (IC) writ large. It includes more than 1,000 declassified CIA clandestine reports and CIA finished intelligence publications. Some of the finished intelligence publications were produced after 1985, but none of the clandestine reports. Although the focus of the study is on the contributions of clandestine human sources, the clandestine and covert technical operations such as the U-2 and satellite reconnaissance programs yielded a treasure trove of information.

BODY-4   *Its unceasing attempts to subvert governments throughout Western Europe and America, and later through the "wars of national liberation" cast a shadow over everyday life in the West.*

BODY-6   *Being convinced that in these circumstances the peace-loving States of Europe must take the necessary steps to safeguard their security and to promote the maintenance of peace in Europe;*

BODY-8   *The decision provides that general questions relating to the strengthening of the defensive power and the organization of the Joint Armed Forces of the signatory states shall be subject to examination by the Political Consultative Committee, which shall adopt the necessary decisions.*

BODY-11   *"Khrushchev's policies affected Soviet internal, political, economic, and military developments. Perhaps most important were his responses to the looming disastrous economic effects of Stalin's legacy, the Sixth Five-Year Plan. To Khrushchev, Stalin's military programs alone required massive misallocation of economic resources. Taken together with the overconcentration of resources for development of heavy industry and inattention to agricultural production, the economy must have looked to Khrushchev like a train heading for a wreck."*

BODY-12   *"Outweighing the promise of a common defense of the Bloc, the Soviet military threat to Poland and the aggression against Hungary represented the downside of the Warsaw Treaty—that it was a formal mechanism for Soviet control."*

BODY-13   *"Richard Helms testifed that 'Lieutenant Colonel Pyotr Popov, until he fell under suspicion, single-handedly supplied the most valuable intelligence on Soviet military matters of any human source available to the United States' during the period. He also said Popov's reporting had a 'direct and signifcant infuence on the military organization of the United States, its doctrine and tactics, and permitted the Pentagon to save at least 500 million dollars in its scientifc research program.'"*

BODY-15   *"The crisis proved to be an important milestone in the development of both NATO and Warsaw Pact military thinking and planning. The strategic importance of what seemed to be overwhelmingly strong Soviet conventional forces facing NATO in Europe became starkly evident to the new US administration of John F. Kennedy. The attempted US responses to the crisis revealed the lack of readiness of the Western forces and underscored the dangers to the West of US reliance on the massive retaliation doctrine for inter-Bloc confrontations short of general (total) war."*

BODY-16   *Khrushchev implicitly threatened to use the massive array of Soviet armored ground forces to prevent the West from protecting its interests in Berlin. He*

	reinforced this threat through large-scale Warsaw Pact exercises conducted in October and November 1961. At the same time, Penkovskiy's reporting indicated the growing concern among the Soviet elite that Khrushchev's threats risked uncontrolled war. Indeed, Penkovskiy reported that the Soviet military hierarchy strongly believed that the Red Army was not ready for a war with NATO over Berlin.
BODY-18	He describes how wars conducted with nuclear weapons will reduce industrialized countries to wastelands in a brief period, thus eliminating the necessity of maintaining large ground forces.
BODY-19	"Te historical prime mission of the Soviet military was the strategic defense of the homeland, focused on massive ground forces and supported by a clearly subordinate navy and air force. Soviet experience during World War II reinforced this concept of military mission. After the elimination of German and Japanese military, the United States stood as the Soviets' principal source of opposition. To bring military power to bear against the United States, Stalin launched a major program to build medium and long range bombers and naval forces."
BODY-20	"Seeing the potential of the nuclear arms as a cheap and flexible means of providing greater security and prominence for the USSR, Khrushchev outlined a new military policy in his report to the Supreme Soviet in January 1960. His plan in essence was to rely mainly on nuclear-missile forces, to reduce military manpower substantially, and to accelerate the retirement of older weapons. This, he asserted, was the force structure best suited both to advance Soviet political and economic interests, and to fight a war when necessary."
BODY-21	"Clandestine reporting by Colonel Penkovskiy provided the first high-level insight into the development of Soviet military hardware and strategy and a wealth of data about the military establishment. Analysts now could determine how the Soviets envisioned their total force from intermediate-range ballistic missiles (IRBMs) to infantry and tank regiments would operate against NATO in Europe."
BODY-23	After the failure of his Berlin gambit and with the US advantage in intercontinental attack capabilities growing, Khrushchev in a break with precedent launched the first major expeditionary force outside the Soviet orbit since WWII. The Soviet plans in May 1962 called for the deploying to Cuba a large number of strategic-range guided missiles with an integrated military force to protect them.
BODY-24	Other information from Penkovskiy provided the basis for the analytical judgments that allowed the United States to calculate reaction times, capabilities, and limitations of the deployed Soviet air defense missile systems. The descriptions and the technical specifications of the "V-75" or SA-2, a surface-to-air missile, and the discussions in the Top Secret 1960–61 special collection Military Thought series about the limitations of the SA-2 and the overall air defense organization disclosed critical Soviet vulnerabilities to high-speed low-level air attack.
BODY-27	"The Secretary of Defense stated that he believed 'the estimates of the strength of the Soviet ground forces...contained in NIE 11-14-62 were overstated.' Referring to the NIE, he wrote that he 'could not understand how the Soviets, with the resources available to them, could have the number of 'well-trained divisions equipped with the excellent materiel' that the IC was estimating they had, when the United States could not afford even half that number of forces.'"
BODY-28	"For the assessment of the personnel strength of the Soviet ground forces by unit or in the aggregate there is no unique type of intelligence source that has as yet become

available. The process is one of gathering fragmentary bits of information in print from which inferences can be drawn with varying degrees of confidence."

BODY-29 After addressing the questions about the quantity of forces, the next all-source analytic challenge was to understand the qualitative distinctions between theory and practice. Secretary McNamara again requested a CIA-DIA team of analysts be brought together. Throughout 1967 and 1968, this team sought better estimates of the capabilities of the Warsaw Pact to mobilize forces and strengthen the area opposite NATO in the central region of Europe. The important question was how well the Soviets could carry out the intentions described in their writings—specifically, how well the divisions were manned and equipped and how well the rear echelons could transport and supply war materiel to combat units in order to meet Soviet requirements for a war with NATO.

BODY-31 "His tactics during the Berlin crisis had failed to bring about control of West Berlin, and he had to abandon his proposal for a separate peace treaty with East Germany. Worse, the Berlin crisis drew the NATO countries closer together and motivated the Western alliance to improve its defenses. Khrushchev's Cuban gamble, moreover, ended in retreat when the United States forced him to remove the missiles. These failures humiliated him and the other Soviet leaders and exposed Soviet strategic inferiority to the world."

BODY-32 "Even so, intelligence collection and analysis during the 1960s suffered from a number of shortcomings. The IC did not know at the beginning of the decade how the Soviets would conduct war with the West, how well they were prepared for such a war, how well their divisions were manned and equipped, how well their rear services transportation capabilities matched wartime requirements, and how well their supplies of war materiel matched their perceptions of the requirements of war with NATO."

BODY-33 "General Secretary Brezhnev (Pravda, 13 November 1968): It is known, comrades, that there are common laws governing socialist construction, a deviation from which might lead to a deviation from socialism as such. And when the internal and external forces hostile to socialism seek to reverse the development of any socialist country toward the restoration of the capitalist order, when a threat to the cause of socialism in that country emerges, a threat to the security of the socialist community as a whole exists; this is no longer a problem of the people of that country but also a common problem, a concern for all socialist states."

BODY-35 Throughout the 1960s and into the 1980s, the decisiveness of strategic nuclear weapons was undisputed among Soviet military theorists. However, by the late 1960s and early 1970s discussions relating to the evolution of military doctrine elaborated on the increased probability that nuclear weapons would not be used in the initial or even later stages of a war with NATO in Europe.

BODY-36 Trough clandestine reporting, CIA military analysts were able to piece together the main elements of Soviet planning for a major air operation at the outset of hostilities with NATO. Classified military journals indicated Soviet military thinkers were on a quest for change in concepts for theater air operations as they sought to evaluate the full significance of the successes of the Israeli and US theater air operations. Later in the decade more evidence became available indicating which changes were actually incorporated in Soviet theater warfare doctrine for air operations.

BODY-37 During approximately the same time period, the US national security establishment had added conventional arms control—Mutual and Balanced Force Reductions (MBFR)—to interests that required more of the IC than ever before.

Policymakers demanded assessments of actual quantities of signature component parts of the forces, not extrapolated estimates. And they wanted more definitive assessments of the qualitative aspects of forces such as training, support, and materiel stocks. Interest in enhancing NATO defenses was also building. Some of the intelligence collection and analysis produced in support of the MBFR effort in effect overturned old assumptions about the Warsaw Pact forces, revealing opportunities for improving NATO defenses.

BODY-58 *The mission of HCD is to: Promote an accurate, objective understanding of the information and intelligence that has helped shape major US foreign policy decisions. Broaden access to lessons-learned, presenting historical material that gives greater understanding to the scope and context of past actions. Improve current decision-making and analysis by facilitating reflection on the impacts and effects arising from past foreign policy decisions. Showcase CIA's contributions to national security and provide the American public with valuable insight into the workings of its government. Demonstrate the CIA's commitment to the Open Government Initiative and its three core values: Transparency, Participation, and Collaboration.*

BODY-60 *The Warsaw Pact contingency plan for war with NATO in the Central Region of Europe – as revised by the Soviets in the early 1960s – assigns the initial offensive missions to the forces already deployed in East Germany, Czechoslovakia, and Poland. In addition, it gives both the Czechs and Poles command over their own national forces. After the initial objectives have been gained, Soviet forces in the western USSR would move quickly into the Central Region and take over the offensive against NATO.*

CIA ANALYSIS OF THE WARSAW PACT FORCES: THE IMPORTANCE OF CLANDESTINE REPORTING

Joan Bird & John Bird
Editors

HISTORICAL COLLECTIONS

Table of Contents

Essay One
CIA Analysis of the Warsaw Pact Forces: The Importance of Clandestine Reporting i

Table of Contents ii

Scope Note 1

Introduction 2

Frequently Used Acronyms 3

The Warsaw Treaty 4
      The Statute of Unified Command 6

Chapter I: **Early Khrushchev Period (1955–60)** **9**
      Organizing and Managing the Warsaw Pact 10
      Intelligence Sources and Analysis in the Early Years 11

Chapter II: **The Berlin Crisis – Col. Oleg Penkovskiy and
Warsaw Pact Preparations for Associated Military Operations (1958–61)** **13**
      Intelligence Sources and Analysis 14

Chapter III: **Soviet Debate on Military Doctrine and Strategy:
The Contribution of Clandestine Source, Col. Oleg Penkovskiy (1955–64)** **17**
      USSR Developments and the Warsaw Pact 17
      Intelligence Sources and Analysis 18

Chapter IV: **New Insights into the Warsaw Pact Forces and Doctrine –
The Cuban Missile Crisis (1962)** **21**
      Khrushchev's Gamble Provides an Intelligence Bonanza 21
      Intelligence Sources and Analysis 21

Chapter V: **New Estimates of the Soviet Ground Forces (1963–68)** **25**
      Defining the Problem 25
      Revising the Estimates of the Strength of Soviet – Warsaw Pact Forces 25
      Clarifying the Estimate of Capabilities and Mobilization of Soviet – Warsaw Pact Forces 27

Chapter VI: **Turmoil in the Soviet Sphere (1962–68)** **29**
      The Demise of Khrushchev 29
      The Brezhnev-Kosygin Team 30
      Managing the Warsaw Pact 30
      Intelligence Sources and Analysis 30

Chapter VII: **Clandestine Reporting and the Analysis and Estimates (1970–85)** **33**
      Soviet-Warsaw Pact Developments and MBFR 33
      Managing the Warsaw Pact 33
      Intelligence Sources and Analysis 34

Essay Two
How Much is Enough? by Alain C. Enthoven 36

Scope Note

This study focuses on the contribution of clandestine source reporting to the production of finished intelligence on the Warsaw Pact's military doctrine, strategy, capabilities, and intentions during the period 1955–85. It examines products of CIA and national intelligence estimates (NIEs) of the Intelligence Community (IC) writ large. It includes more than 1,000 declassified CIA clandestine reports and CIA finished intelligence publications. Some of the finished intelligence publications were produced after 1985, but none of the clandestine reports. Although the focus of the study is on the contributions of clandestine human sources, the clandestine and covert technical operations such as the U-2 and satellite reconnaissance programs yielded a treasure trove of information that was incorporated in CIA's analysis. Chapter V illustrates the special significance of those reconnaissance programs for the solution of some important problems in the 1960s but those programs yielded essential information throughout the thirty year period studied.

The analytical reports featured in the study are generally the results of long-term research using all sources of information. With some exceptions, the study excludes CIA current intelligence reporting. Nor does it address intelligence on Warsaw Pact naval forces or Soviet strategic forces, the great contributions of signals intelligence (SIGINT), or intelligence from the US Army, Navy, or Air Force. The services' intelligence components played important roles, for example, as the principal contributors to the military-focused NIEs for the period 1955–61, with the exception of the military-related economic and scientific estimating and in accord with the National Security Council Intelligence Directives (NSCID)[1] of the time. This study also does not specifically address the contributions of economic, political, weapons, or scientific intelligence efforts, but it does, as appropriate attend to the operational and strategic consequences of those efforts. It only generally discusses intelligence support for the Mutual and Balanced Force Reductions (MBFR) negotiations.

The study refers to many documents provided by clandestine sources; these references are generally meant to be illustrative, not exhaustive. Finally, the study includes historical material to provide a general context for discussing the intelligence. It is not intended, however, to be a definitive history of the times.

The authors owe a debt of gratitude to the many intelligence officers who painstakingly sifted through the not always well-organized archives for documents sometimes 50 or more years old. They especially note the assistance of officers of the Defense Intelligence Agency (DIA) for searching their archives for CIA reports the authors were unable to locate in CIA archives.

> This essay was produced by Joan and John Bird.

[1] See NSCID No.3, Coordination of Intelligence Production, 13 January 1948, and NSCID No. 3, Coordination of Intelligence Production, 21 April 1958 for details of the responsibilities of the CIA and other intelligence departments and agencies of the US government. NSCID No. 3 limited the role of CIA to economic and scientific analysis, making the military services responsible for all military intelligence. The 1958 revised version broadened the areas for which the CIA could produce intelligence.

Session of the Council of Ministers of the Warsaw Treaty Member States, December 1981

Introduction

The Soviet Union established itself as a threat to the West by its military occupation of Poland and other eastern European countries at the end of World War II and through the unsuccessful attempts by its armed proxies to capture Greece and South Korea. Its unceasing attempts to subvert governments throughout Western Europe and America, and later through the "wars of national liberation" cast a shadow over everyday life in the West. The massive Soviet armed forces stationed in central Europe stood behind its political offensives such as the Berlin Crises. The West countered with the formation of NATO and the acceptance into NATO, and rebuilding of, West Germany. During the same period that the West welcomed West Germany into NATO, the Soviets established – through the Warsaw Treaty of May 1955 – a formal military bloc of Communist nations.

This study continues CIA's effort to provide the public with a more detailed record of the intelligence derived from clandestine human and technical sources that was provided to US policymakers and used to assess the political and military balances and confrontations in Central Europe between the Warsaw Pact and NATO during the Cold War. Finished intelligence[2], based on human and technical sources, was the basis for personal briefings of the President, Vice President, Secretary of Defense, Secretary of State, and other cabinet members, and for broader distribution through NIEs. It is the opinion of the authors that the information considerably aided US efforts to preserve the peace at a bearable cost.

This study showcases the importance of clandestine source reporting to CIA's analysis of the Warsaw Pact forces. This effort complements the CIA's release of the "Caesar" series of studies[3] and other significant CIA documents in 2007; and releases by other IC agencies. It also complements ongoing projects, including those of the Wilson Center of the Smithsonian Institution and NATO that reexamine the Cold War in light of newly available documentation released by several former members of the Warsaw Pact.

The clandestine reports by the predecessor organizations of CIA's current National Clandestine Service (NCS) are representative of those that at the time made especially valuable contributions to understanding the history, plans, and intentions of the Warsaw Pact. Many of these documents are being released for the first time. The clandestine source documents do not represent a complete record of contemporary intelligence collection. There was much information made available from émigrés and defectors as well as from imagery and SIGINT that was essential in the estimative process but is not the focus of this study.

The study includes NIEs that CIA has previously released. It also includes finished intelligence documents produced by the CIA's Directorate of Intelligence (DI), some previously released, and the clandestinely obtained information upon which those reports were largely based. The DI reports were selected in part because they were the detailed basis of CIA contributions to NIEs that focused on the military aspects of the Warsaw Pact. The DI finished intelligence reports also provided the background for future current intelligence. Appended to this study is a collection of declassified intelligence documents relating to the Warsaw Pact's military forces, operational planning, and capabilities. Although many of the documents were released in past years, new reviews have provided for the restoration of text previously redacted. All of the documents selected for this study are available on the attached DVD, on CIA's website at **http://www.foia.cia.gov/special_collections.asp** or from the CIA Records Search Tool (CREST) located at the National Archives and Records Administration (NARA), College Park, MD or contact us at **HistoricalCollections@UCIA.gov**.

The finished intelligence during this period seldom linked the specific clandestine or other sources of evidence to the analysis based on their information. For example, the early intelligence documents often described clandestine sources only in the most general fashion. Rules to protect sources, especially the human agents, rarely allowed analysts to acknowledge a clandestine source, openly evaluate a source's reliability, or describe a source's access to the information. Only in publications of extremely limited distribution, for as few as a handful of recipients, were these rules relaxed. They changed little until the 1980s, when analysts could provide evaluations that included some sense of the source's reliability and access.

The study lists in the Catalogue of Documents on the DVD important clandestine and covert source reports and finished intelligence publications by chapter. These documents are generally arrayed chronologically according to the dates of dissemination within the IC, not the dates of publication by the Soviets that sometimes were years earlier.

> All of our Historical Collections are available on the CIA Library Publication page located at https://www.cia.gov/library/publications/historical-collection-publications/ or contact us at HistoricalCollections@UCIA.gov.

---

[2] Finished Intelligence is the CIA term for the product resulting from the collection, processing, integration, analysis, evaluation, and interpretation of available all source information. [3] The Caesar Studies are analytic monographs and reference aids produced by the DI through the 1950s to the mid-1970s. They provided in-depth research on Soviet internal politics primarily intended to give insight on select political and economic issues and CIA analytic thinking of the period.

Frequently Used Acronyms

CPSU/CC	Communist Party of the Soviet Union Central Committee
CSI	Center for the Study of Intelligence
DCI	Director of Central Intelligence
DIA	Defense Intelligence Agency
DI	Directorate of Intelligence (CIA)
DO	Directorate of Operations, 1973–2005 (CIA)
DP	Directorate of Plans, 1950s–1973 (CIA)
FBIS	Foreign Broadcast Information Service
FRG	Federal Republic of Germany (West Germany)
FRUS	Foreign Relations of the United States (A US Department of State History Series)
GDR	German Democratic Republic (East Germany)
IC	Intelligence Community
MBFR	Mutual and Balanced Force Reductions
NARA	National Archives and Records Administration
NCS	National Clandestine Service, 2005–present (CIA)
NIC	National Intelligence Council, established December 1979 (DCI)
NIC/WC	National Indications Center/Watch Committee, pre-1979 (DCI)
NIE	National Intelligence Estimate
NPIC	National Photographic Interpretation Center
NSCID	National Security Council Intelligence Directive
NSC	National Security Council
NSWP	Non-Soviet Warsaw Pact [countries]
NTM	National Technical Means
OCI	Office of Current Intelligence (CIA
OER	Office of Economic Research (CIA
ONE	Office of National Estimates (CIA
OPA	Office of Political Analysis (CIA)
ORR	Office of Research and Reports (C
OSR	Office of Strategic Research (CIA)
PCC	Political Consultative Committee (
SOVA	Office of Soviet Analysis (CIA)
SHAPE	Supreme Headquarters Allied Pow
SIGINT	Signals Intelligence
SNIE	Special National Intelligence Estim
SRS	Senior Research Staff
TO&E	Table of Organization and Equipm
WMD	Weapons of Mass Destruction

The Warsaw Treaty

The founding document of the Warsaw Pact organization was signed in Warsaw on 14 May 1955, and came into force on 6 June 1955. At the time, CIA analysts judged that Moscow had drafted the treaty without consulting its allies and had modeled it after the 1949 North Atlantic Treaty (sometimes referred to as the Washington Treaty) that established NATO. CIA analysis showed that some clauses of the Warsaw Treaty appeared to be almost direct translations from the Washington Treaty and that both had similar provisions, for example, for joint action in case one of the signatories was attacked, recognition of the ultimate authority of the UN, and settlement of all disputes without use or threat of force. The combined military command seemed to be a facsimile of NATO's Supreme Headquarters Allied Powers Europe (SHAPE).[4] The treaty apparently was not crafted to override existing bilateral treaties of mutual assistance, friendship, and cooperation between Moscow and its allies, which were the basis for addressing Soviet security concerns in Europe at that time. CIA analysts believed that the Warsaw Treaty was set up primarily as a bargaining chip to obtain the dissolution of NATO. The following text of the treaty does not include the signature blocks.

Treaty of Friendship, Cooperation, and Mutual Assistance between the People's Republic of Albania, the People's Republic of Bulgaria, the Hungarian People's Republic, the German Democratic Republic, the Polish People's Republic, the Romanian Socialist Republic, the Union of Soviet Socialist Republics, and the Czechoslovak Republic.[5]

The Contracting Parties

Reaffirming their desire to create a system of collective security in Europe based on the participation of all European States, irrespective their social and political structure, whereby the said States may be enabled to combine their efforts in the interests of ensuring peace in Europe;

Taking into consideration, at the same time, the situation that has come about in Europe as a result of the ratification of the Paris Agreements, which provide for the constitution of a new military group in the form of a "West European Union", with the participation of a remilitarized West Germany and its inclusion in the North Atlantic bloc, thereby increasing the danger of a new war and creating a threat to the national security of peace-loving States;

Being convinced that in these circumstances the peace-loving States of Europe must take the necessary steps to safeguard their security and to promote the maintenance of peace in Europe;

Being guided by the purposes and principles of the Charter of the United Nations Organization;

In the interests of further strengthening and development of friendship, co-operation and mutual assistance in accordance with the principles of respect for the independence and sovereignty of States and of non-intervention in their domestic affairs;

Have resolved to conclude the present Treaty of Friendship, Co-operation and Mutual Assistance and have appointed as their plenipotentiaries: [not listed here]

who, having exhibited their full powers, found in good and due form, have agreed as follows:

Article 1

The Contracting Parties undertake, in accordance with the Charter of the United Nations Organization, to refrain in their international relations from the threat or use of force, and to settle their international disputes by peaceful means in such a manner that international peace and security are not endangered.

Article 2

The Contracting Parties declare that they are prepared to participate, in a spirit of sincere co-operation in all international action for ensuring international peace and security, and will devote their full efforts to the realization of these aims.
In this connexion, the Contracting Parties shall endeavor to secure, in agreement with other states desiring to co-operate in this matter, the adoption of effective measures for the general reduction of armaments and the prohibition of atomic, hydrogen and other weapons of mass destruction

Article 3

The Contracting Parties shall consult together on all important international questions involving their common interests, with a view to strengthening international peace and security.

Whenever any one of the Contracting Parties considers that a threat of armed attack on one or more of the States Parties to the Treaty has arisen, they shall consult together immediately with a view to providing for their joint defense and maintaining peace and security.

---

[4] A comparison of the Warsaw Treaty with the 1949 Washington Treaty establishing NATO can be found in a study prepared by the CIA's Office of Current Intelligence 22 years later, *The Warsaw Pact: Its Role in Soviet Bloc Affairs from Its Origin to the Present Day*, A Study for the Jackson Subcommittee, 5 May 1966 (See the Catalogue of Documents, Chapter VI, Document VI-13, Annex B, p B-1. [5] The text of the treaty was available through the FBIS Daily Report on 14 May 1955, but we do not have a copy of that report. The text of the treaty here is a UN English translation of the text of the treaty as registered at the UN by Poland on 10 October 1955.

Article 4

In the event of an armed attack in Europe on one or more of the States Parties to the Treaty by any state or group of States, each State Party to the Treaty, shall, in the exercise of the right of individual or collective self-defense, in accordance with Article 51 of the United Nations Charter, afford the State or States so attacked immediate assistance, individually and in agreement with the other States Parties to the Treaty, by all means it considers necessary, including the use of armed force. The States Parties to the Treaty shall consult together immediately concerning the joint measures necessary to restore and maintain international peace and security.

Measures taken under this Article shall be reported to the Security Council in accordance with the provisions of the United Nations Charter. These measures shall be discontinued as soon as the Security Council takes the necessary action to restore and maintain international peace and security.

Article 5

The Contracting Parties have agreed to establish a Unified Command, to which certain elements of their armed forces shall be allocated by agreement between the parties, and which shall act in accordance with jointly established principles. The Parties shall likewise take such other concerted action as may be necessary to reinforce their defensive strength, in order to defend the peaceful labour of their peoples, guarantee the inviolability of their frontiers and territories and afford protection against possible aggression.

Article 6

For the purpose of carrying out the consultations provided for in the present Treaty between the States Parties thereto, and for the consideration of matters arising in connexion with the application of the present Treaty, a Political Consultative Committee shall be established, in which each State Party to the Treaty shall be represented by a member of the government or by some other specially appointed representative.

The Committee may establish such auxiliary organs as may prove to be necessary.

Article 7

The Contracting Parties undertake not to participate in any coalitions or alliances and not to conclude any agreements the purposes of which are incompatible with the purposes of the present Treaty.

The Contracting Parties declare that their obligations under international treaties at present in force are not incompatible with the provisions of the present Treaty.

Article 8

The Contracting Parties declare that they will act in a spirit of friendship and co-operation to promote the further development and strengthening of the economic and cultural ties among them, in accordance with the principles of respect for each other's independence and sovereignty and of non-intervention in each other's domestic affairs.

Article 9

The present Treaty shall be open for accession by other States, irrespective of their social and political structure, which express their readiness, by participating in the present Treaty, to help in combining the efforts of the peace-loving states to ensure the peace and security of the peoples. Such accessions shall come into effect with the consent of the States Parties to the Treaty after the instruments of accession have been deposited with the Government of the Polish People's Republic.

Article 10

The present Treaty shall be subject to ratification, and the instruments of ratification shall be deposited with the Government of the Polish People's Republic.

The Treaty shall come into force on the date of deposit of the last instrument of ratification. The Government of the Polish People's Republic shall inform the other States Parties to the Treaty of the deposit of each instrument of ratification.

Article 11

The present Treaty shall remain in force for twenty years. For contracting Parties which do not, one year before the expiration of that term, give notice of termination of the treaty to the government of the Polish People's Republic, the Treaty shall remain in force for a further ten years.

In the event of the establishment of a system of collective security in Europe and the conclusion for that purpose of a General European Treaty concerning collective security, a goal which the Contracting Parties shall steadfastly strive to achieve, the Treaty shall cease to have effect as from the date on which the General European Treaty comes into force.

Done at Warsaw, this fourteenth day of May 1955, in one copy, in the Russian, Polish, Czech and German languages, all texts being equally authentic. Certified copies of the present Treaty shall be transmitted by the Government of the Polish People's Republic to all other Parties to the Treaty.

In witness whereof the plenipotentiaries have signed the present Treaty and affixed their seals.

The Statute on Unified Command

A Statute on Unified Command was completed on 7 September 1955, but not approved, signed or ratified until March 18, 1980. It was kept secret by the USSR and was not available to CIA analysts in 1955.

The Establishment of a Combined Command of the Armed Forces of the Signatories to the Treaty of Friendship, Cooperation and Mutual Assistance.[6]

In pursuance of the Treaty of Friendship, Cooperation and Mutual Assistance between the People's Republic of Albania, the People's Republic of Bulgaria, the Hungarian People's Republic, the German Democratic Republic, the Polish People's Republic, the Rumanian People's Republic, the Union of Soviet Socialist Republics and the Czechoslovak Republic, the signatory states have decided to establish a Combined Command of their armed forces.

> The decision provides that general questions relating to the strengthening of the defensive power and the organization of the Joint Armed Forces of the signatory states shall be subject to examination by the Political Consultative Committee, which shall adopt the necessary decisions.
>
> Marshal of the Soviet Union I.S. Konev has been appointed Commander-in-Chief of the Joint Armed Forces to be assigned by the signatory states.
>
> The Ministers of Defense or other military leaders of the signatory states are to serve as Deputy Commanders-in-Chief of the Joint Armed Forces, and shall command the armed forces assigned by their respective states to the Joint Armed Forces.
>
> The question of the participation of the German Democratic Republic in measures concerning the armed forces of the Joint Command will be examined at a later date.
>
> A Staff of the Joint Armed Forces of the signatory states will be set up under the Commander-in-Chief of the Joint Armed Forces, and will include permanent representatives of the General Staffs of the signatory states.
>
> The Staff will have its headquarters in Moscow.
>
> The disposition of the Joint Armed Forces in the territories of the signatory states will be effected by agreement among the states, in accordance with the requirement of their mutual defense.[7]

---

6 Ibid, Catalogue, Document VI-13, see Annex A, p A-5. **7** For additional information about the fate of this statute, see the Catalogue of Documents, Document VII-177.

CIA ANALYSIS OF THE WARSAW PACT FORCES: THE IMPORTANCE OF CLANDESTINE REPORTING

Warsaw Pact Countries, 1955–1991

Warsaw Pact

Albania*	Hungary
Bulgaria	Poland
Czechoslovakia	Romania
East Germany	U.S.S.R.

*Albania withheld support in 1961 over the China split and officially withdrew in 1968.

UNCLASSIFIED

CHAPTER I

Early Khrushchev Period (1955-1960)

Changes in Soviet relations with the West after the death of Stalin and the consolidation of power by Nikita Khrushchev[8] initially characterized this period. By deed and word Moscow offered prospects for détente. At the same time Khrushchev attempted to bully the West by exploiting the purported strength of Soviet military and economic superiority. Soviet actions included the signing of the Vienna Agreement (known formally as the Austrian State Treaty) freeing Austria of Soviet controls, which contrasted with his threats to "bury" the West, and explicit military confrontation over Berlin and Cuba between 1958 and 1962. Advances in military-related technologies as well as the changing relationships between the Soviet and Western Blocs also led to internal debates and changes in national military strategies beginning first in the West and later in and among the Warsaw Pact countries and the Soviet Union.

Khrushchev's policies affected Soviet internal, political, economic, and military developments. Perhaps most important were his responses to the looming disastrous economic effects of Stalin's legacy, the Sixth Five-Year Plan. To Khrushchev, Stalin's military programs alone required massive misallocation of economic resources. Taken together with the overconcentration of resources for development of heavy industry and inattention to agricultural production, the economy must have looked to Khrushchev like a train heading for a wreck. He instituted a major reorganization of the bureaucracy to control the economy including huge new agricultural programs, and substituted a new Seven-Year Plan for the doomed Sixth Five-Year Plan.[9]

On 15 May 1955, the United States, United Kingdom, France, and the Soviet Union signed the Vienna Agreement, which provided for the withdrawal of the Soviet and Western forces from Austria. This show of confidence on the part of the Soviets was followed by Khrushchev's August 1955 announcement of a reduction of 640,000 men from the Soviet armed forces. In May 1956 he called for another cutback of 1.2 million Soviet troops. In 1957, in a climax to maneuvering by military and political leadership for power, Khrushchev ousted Minister of Defense Marshal Zhukov and reestablished party control of the military. He also began retiring senior Soviet military officers who disagreed with his policies. Khrushchev reorganized the Soviet military[10] and promoted those officers who supported his pronouncements on the nature of a war with NATO. He advocated military capabilities with which he believed wars would be fought. These actions and his fixation on missiles and planning for nuclear war took center stage by 1961 when a debate took place among Soviet military officers that was reflected in special Top Secret Editions of *Military Thought*.[11]

Khrushchev later announced additional unilateral troop reductions including one of 300,000 troops in January 1958 and another of 1.2 million in January 1960 in a speech to the Supreme Soviet. All of the proposed decreases were meant to serve several purposes: to shift funds into the production of missiles and long-range bombers; to lessen the burden of ground force requirements on heavy industry; to free labor for productive purposes in the civilian economy; and to bring international pressure on the United States to cut its forces. The aim of the reductions proposed in 1960 and in the years immediately following also may have been to compensate for the smaller numbers of militarily acceptable men available to the armed services, because of the low birth rate attendant to the tremendous losses suffered during World War II (WWII).

---

8 Khrushchev became First Secretary of the CPSU/CC in March 1953 and Premier in March 1958. **9** The editors have drawn from the documents listed in the Catalogue of Documents for each chapter for much of the material in the chapter essays. References in the essays to material drawn from documents listed in other chapters are noted in footnotes. **10** For more information on the reorganization of the Soviet Army, see the Catalogue of Documents, Document VII-91, Organizational Development of the Soviet Ground Forces, 1957-1975, 7–14. **11** See FBIS Radio Propaganda Reports addressing the debates among the military leadership that appeared in the open press following the death of Stalin in 1953. The debates also were addressed in secret and top secret versions of the Soviet military journal, *Military Thought* that are addressed in Chapter III.

Organizing and Managing the Warsaw Pact

The Twentieth CPSU Congress in February 1956, famous for Khrushchev's anti-Stalin speech, ushered in what would become an era of many changes in Soviet–East European relations. The congress set forth new guidance for communist governance, implicit and explicit, and dissolved the COMINFORM[12] to "facilitate cooperation with the socialist parties" of the noncommunist world. The resulting policy vacuum in Eastern Europe persisted though the fall of 1956 and probably was an important precipitant of the Hungarian uprising and the riots in Poland. Intentionally or not, Khrushchev's condemnation of Stalinism unsettled the communist governments of Eastern Europe, most of which were run by unreconstructed Stalinists. Their ousting from office was accompanied by unintended disorder and some violent outbreaks of worker discontent in Eastern Europe that the presence of Soviet garrisons could not avert. Subsequent actions would illustrate that Moscow's guidance for communist governance notwithstanding, the Warsaw Treaty was providing a new vehicle for establishing Soviet authority over intra-Bloc relations. Moscow defined this authority even to include "legitimizing" physical intervention, a vehicle that the Soviets would soon use.

By midsummer 1956, riots in Poland threatened the future integrity and success of the year-old Warsaw Pact. The Soviets mobilized and prepared forces in response, but the crisis was resolved short of Soviet military intervention. Instead, the Soviets employed those forces to suppress the far more serious situation developing in Hungary, after the Hungarians forcibly removed the remnants of the oppressive Stalinist regime and installed the mildly communist one of Imre Nagy. Nagy opted to lead Hungary out of the Warsaw Pact, treason in the eyes of the Soviets. After the garrison of Soviet forces in Hungary initially took a beating at the hands of the revolutionaries, the Soviets unleashed the forces mobilized to intervene in Poland. The bloody suppression that ensued reimposed Soviet control. In a declaration on 30 October 1956, Moscow hypocritically stated its readiness to respect the sovereignty of its Warsaw Pact allies even as the Soviets already were in the process of violating Hungary's.

Outweighing the promise of a common defense of the Bloc, the Soviet military threat to Poland and the aggression against Hungary represented the downside of the Warsaw Treaty—that it was a formal mechanism for Soviet control. The rocky start for the Warsaw Pact was followed by the growing estrangement of Albania and Romania, and problems with China. Yugoslavia had already bolted from the Soviet orbit in 1948. Nonetheless, the Soviets persevered, building the Warsaw Treaty Organization into an ever-tightening device for controlling its satellite allies, and a source of additional military power.

In broad general terms, the Soviet General Staff created the Warsaw Pact military plans even though the Warsaw Treaty provided formal arrangements for the Soviets and their East European allies to share management of their combined military forces. Contrary to the Articles of the Warsaw Treaty, particularly Article 5, Soviet planning for the Warsaw Pact initially called for the forces of non-Soviet Warsaw Pact (NSWP) countries to remain under nominal national control, with the intention that the Soviets would closely direct all forces during a crisis or war. Nonetheless, throughout the life of the Warsaw Pact, the NSWP members, with varying degrees of success, resisted yielding control of their own forces to Soviet unilateral command. Only in the case of East German forces did the Soviets fully succeed.

During the 1950s CIA analysts assessed that the Warsaw Pact's forces were not integrated and jointly controlled and that only the Soviets really managed them. The IC in NIE 11-4-58, *Main Trends in Soviet Capabilities and Policies, 1958-1963*, judged it unlikely that Soviet planners would count on East European forces to make an important contribution to Soviet military operations except perhaps for air defense. Soviet preparations for military contingencies associated with Moscow's projected aggressive moves against West Berlin in the summer of 1961 called for putting all NSWP forces into Soviet field armies, clearly a plan to subordinate the former to Soviet control.

After the dissolution of the Warsaw Pact, archival documents from former members further illustrated their unequal treatment during this period. In a 1956 classified critique of the statute of the Unified Command, Polish Gen. Jan Drzewiecki complained, "The document in its present form grants the Supreme Commander of the Unified Armed Forces certain rights and obligations, which contradict the idea of the independence and sovereignty of the member states of the Warsaw Treaty."[13] In a January 1957 *Memorandum on Reform of the Warsaw Pact*, General Drzewiecki further stated, "The authority of the Supreme Commander [a Soviet officer] on questions of leadership in combat and strategic training is incompatible with the national character of the armies of the corresponding states."[14] In the latter half of the 1970s Col. Ryszard Kuklinski, a CIA clandestine source, provided information revealing the NSWP members finally signed and ratified the Statutes on 18 March 1978, except for the one on Unified Command for Wartime. That one was not signed and ratified until 1980.[15] Clearly the Soviets had not achieved their aims at legal control for decades.

---

12 COMINFORM was the acronym for the "Information Bureau of the Communist and Worker's Parties" that was founded in 1947. Its purpose was to coordinate the foreign policy activities of the East European communist parties under Soviet direction. **13** *A Cardboard Castle? An Inside History of the Warsaw Pact 1955-1991*, edited by Vojtech Mastny and Malcolm Byrne, Central European University Press, Budapest, New York, p.84–86. **14** Ibid, 87–90. **15** See Chapter VII, page 35 for more details on the statutes. For the documents, see the Catalogue of Documents, Chapter 7, Section, "Formal Mechanisms to Manage the Warsaw Pact," page 185.

Intelligence Sources and Analysis in the Early Years

The Western Allies shared military and policy information to a limited extent with the Soviet Union during WWII, but even that all but ceased when the war ended. By 1949, the Soviet Union and its allies were concealing much of their military activities and policy decisions from the outside world. The police state that Stalin established made recruiting human sources inside the USSR extremely difficult[16] and prevented Western diplomats and military attachés from traveling widely there. Thus, the central problem for CIA analysts during this period of the Cold War in Europe was the lack of direct and convincing evidence other than that derived from SIGINT, defectors, and the media. Efforts to fill the gaps in collection with photography and other supporting information were of limited success.

In the early 1950s military analysts based their understanding of Soviet military organization, doctrine, capabilities, and tactics largely on evidence from World War II, SIGINT, information available from the Soviet press, military attaché reporting, defector and émigré debriefings, and the observations of US military missions in Austria and East Germany. Some German prisoners of the Soviet Union from the WWII period and some Spanish émigrés from the Spanish Civil War days who were returning to the West provided valuable military-industrial information. For example, the German prisoners, who had worked on Hitler's missile program and were forced to help the Soviet program, relayed useful data about Soviet missile programs. Most Soviet military émigrés or defectors, however, were generally low level and the military defectors could report only on their experiences in the military units where they served—typically located in Austria or East Germany.

During the period 1955–59, CIA had only two productive clandestine sources of Soviet military information. One was a special project, the Berlin Tunnel Operation, which yielded invaluable information, for example, about deployed military forces, Soviet political-military relationships, and the tactical-level organization and manning of Soviet forces in East Germany through most of 1955 until spring 1956.[17] The other was Major (later promoted to Lt. Colonel) Pyotr Popov, the CIA's first high-quality clandestine Soviet military source.

Popov served in place and reported on Soviet military policy, doctrine, strategy, tactics and organization from 1953 until the late 1950s. Richard Helms testified that "Lieutenant Colonel Pyotr Popov, until he fell under suspicion, single-handedly supplied the most valuable intelligence on Soviet military matters of any human source available to the United States" during the period.[18] He also said Popov's reporting had a "direct and significant influence on the military organization of the United States, its doctrine and tactics, and permitted the Pentagon to save at least 500 million dollars in its scientific research program."[19] The information and documents he provided continued to inform the CIA analysis years after he was arrested.

Popov provided the IC with unique classified documentary and semi-documentary information otherwise unavailable after the late 1940s, including extant Field Service Regulations of the Armed Forces of the USSR and other manuals that provided new doctrine and strategies for the armed forces.[20] The subjects of his reports ranged from routine unit locations to nuclear warfare tactics, strategic air operations, and guided missiles. He supplied the IC with information on the organization and functions of the Soviet General Staff and technical specifications of Soviet Army conventional weapons, including the first information about new weapons such as the T-10 heavy tank and PT-76 amphibious light tank. Popov also provided documents on Khrushchev's reorganization of the Soviet military and a number of unique and highly valuable classified documents of the Communist Party of the Soviet Union Central Committee (CPSU/CC), including those concerning Soviet policy toward Berlin. The information Popov supplied was important for understanding the Soviet political and military establishments following the Stalinist years and at the startup of the Warsaw Pact. And it provided a basis for understanding how the political and military establishments of the satellite countries would operate with the Soviet Union. Because of the tight control over disseminated information from the Popov operation, analysts made no references in finished intelligence that might lead to his apprehension. However, much later, a former officer in the CIA's Directorate of Plans (DP), William Hood, in his 1982 book, *Mole*,[21] extensively discussed Popov's contribution.

According to CIA records, Popov also supplied copies of the Soviet military publication, *Military Thought*.[22] We know from the author of a CIA study, *Soviet Naval Strategy and the Effect on the Development of the Naval Forces 1953-1963*, that *Military Thought* articles from the 1953–59 period were available for his analysis. Analysts who participated in the 1963 CIA/DIA joint study, discussed in Chapter V,[23] also had Popov-supplied documents available to support their analysis. The above testimony shows that his efforts provided the IC with some of the best human-source information on developing Soviet military tactics and doctrine during the period.

---

16 For more information on the difficulties in recruiting Soviet human sources during the early years, see William Hood, *Mole, The True Story of the First Russian Intelligence Officer Recruited by the CIA*, (New York: W.W. Norton and Company, 1982). **17** For more information on the Berlin Tunnel project see Catalogue of Documents, Document I-34 the official *Clandestine Services History, The Berlin Tunnel Operation 1952-1956, 24 June 1968*; for information on the intelligence derived from the Berlin Project, see Annex B, "Recapitulation of the Intelligence Derived". Also see Donald P. Steury, ed., *On the Front Lines of the Cold War: Documents on the Intelligence War in Berlin, 1946 to 1961* (Washington, DC: Center for the Study of Intelligence, 1999). **18** See Richard Helms, with William Hood, *A Look over My Shoulder A Life in the Central Intelligence Agency* (New York: Random House, 2003), 105. **19** Ibid. Helms p.132. **20** See Catalogue of Documents, Document III-11, *Military Thought*, Issue No.1, 1964, "The New Field Service Regulations of the Armed Forces of the USSR, for a discussion by Marshal Chuykov on the importance of the Field Service Regulation Manuals for putting into effect new doctrine and strategies for the armed forces. **21** Hood, *Mole*. **22** NARA has available fourteen Russian-language issues of *Military Thought* from the period 1953–58, when Popov was active. **23** For references to documents provided by Popov that aided the Joint CIA/DIA study, See the Catalogue of Documents, Document V-13, p. 54, *A Study of the Soviet Ground Forces, An Interim Report of the CIA-DIA Panel for a Special Study of the Soviet Ground Forces for Secretary McNamara*, 21 August 1963.

CHAPTER II

The Berlin Crisis—Col. Oleg Penkovskiy and Warsaw Pact Preparations for Associated Military Operations (1958–1961)

The second Berlin crisis was a continuation of the disagreement over the future of Germany and Berlin that caused the first crisis in 1948. The seeds of both were sown in discussions during WWII over who would eventually control Germany and Berlin. The Allied powers—the United States, Great Britain, and the Soviet Union—agreed in 1944 on joint occupation and administration of the country and its capital. This arrangement was formalized in June 1945, after Germany had surrendered, and a fourth sector of occupation was established for France. The agreement provided the three Western powers with the right of access to Berlin, located deep within the Soviet-controlled part of Germany that later became the German Democratic Republic (GDR).[24] In an attempt to abrogate the agreement over the city, the Soviets walked out of the first Allied Control Council in 1948, declaring that the Western powers no longer had any rights to administer Berlin. By 23 June, the Soviets had completely blocked deliveries of food and other supplies over land to the three Western-controlled sectors of the city. Thus began the first Berlin crisis. The Western powers responded with a huge operation, known as the Berlin Airlift, flying in 4,000 tons of supplies a day to the city until the Soviets lifted the blockade in May 1949.

After the crisis subsided the Soviets continued to harass Allied military truck convoys to West Berlin from West Germany. In the meantime, the United States, France and the United Kingdom began establishing a nucleus for a future German government that eventually became the Federal Republic of Germany (FRG). Khrushchev instigated a second crisis on 10 November 1958. At the Friendship Meeting of the Peoples of the Soviet Union and Poland, he delivered what was in effect an ultimatum calling for a separate peace treaty with the GDR that would terminate the Western powers' right of access to West Berlin. After the speech, relations between the United States and the Soviet Union deteriorated sharply, and a series of political and military confrontations over the status of Berlin followed. The crisis culminated in the building of the Berlin Wall in August 1961 and with US and Soviet armored forces facing off directly against each other at Checkpoint Charlie on the border between East and West Berlin. As in the crisis of 1948, the Soviets sought to force the West to abandon control of the Western sectors of Berlin and to stop the flow of East German refugees. CIA analysis judged Khrushchev evidently also hoped that forcing the Western powers to recognize East Germany and leave Berlin would discredit the United States as the defender of the West and eventually cause NATO to dissolve.

The crisis proved to be an important milestone in the development of both NATO and Warsaw Pact military thinking and planning. The strategic importance of what seemed to be overwhelmingly strong Soviet conventional forces facing NATO in Europe became starkly evident to the new US administration of John F. Kennedy. The attempted US responses to the crisis revealed the lack of readiness of the Western forces and underscored the dangers to the West of US reliance on the massive retaliation doctrine for inter-Bloc confrontations short of general (total) war. The crisis was perhaps the greatest test of the solidarity and meaning of NATO since the Berlin Airlift.[25] It threatened to lead to direct conventional military hostilities between NATO and the Warsaw Pact ground forces that could easily escalate to nuclear warfare.

---

24 Op cit. *On the Front Lines*, Preface and Introduction, pp iii, v, 131-135. See also *Foreign Relations of the United States (FRUS)*, 1948, Germany and Austria, Volume II, Chapter IV, "The Berlin Crisis", pages 867–1284, for more detailed information on this period of post-WWII Four Power occupation and administration of Germany and the ensuing crisis. The early FRUS volumes are available through the Library website of the University of Wisconsin. **25** For a brief summary of the discussions in August 1961 of how Western countries saw future developments of the Berlin situation and how they proposed to handle it, see *Foreign Relations of the United States (FRUS)* Vol. XIV, 372–73. The term, "Live Oak", which appears in the FRUS discussion, was the code name for Western Quadripartite Powers' planning for a military confrontation within the larger context of NATO war planning.

CIA ANALYSIS OF THE WARSAW PACT FORCES: THE IMPORTANCE OF CLANDESTINE REPORTING

Intelligence Sources and Analysis

Col. Oleg Penkovskiy, a Soviet officer who became a clandestine source of CIA and the British MI-6, began reporting in April 1961 about Khrushchev's views of the Kennedy administration, and subsequently supplied invaluable insights into Khrushchev's plans and military capabilities for confronting the West over Berlin.

Khrushchev implicitly threatened to use the massive array of Soviet armored ground forces to prevent the West from protecting its interests in Berlin. He reinforced this threat through large-scale Warsaw Pact exercises conducted in October and November 1961. At the same time, Penkovskiy's reporting indicated the growing concern among the Soviet elite that Khrushchev's threats risked uncontrolled war. Indeed, Penkovskiy reported that the Soviet military hierarchy strongly believed that the Red Army was not ready for a war with NATO over Berlin.[26]

During the summer and fall of 1961 CIA continued to disseminate reports based on information surreptitiously passed by Penkovskiy and elicited at clandestine meetings during his trips to England and France. The reports almost certainly bolstered the President's resolve to take strong military actions to counter any Soviet attempts to force change in the status of Berlin. The reports also showed growing Soviet concern about US and NATO intentions toward Berlin. According to the clandestine information, Moscow ordered Soviet embassies in all capitalist countries to determine the degree of participation of each NATO country in decisions about Berlin.

Because of the extreme sensitivity of the source, little was written down about the precise communication of Penkovskiy's information to the President. Circumstantial evidence suggests Penkovskiy's reporting was an important unrecorded motivation in US policy councils. It was certainly prescient regarding Soviet reaction to the US decisions. CIA does have evidence that DCI Allen Dulles briefed the President on 14 July 1961 and that Penkovskiy's reporting was read by the President as he prepared his 25 July speech to the American people. CIA also has evidence that Penkovskiy's reporting was sent to the White House for a morning briefing on 22 August and that his reporting was pouched to the President in Newport, RI, in September 1961.

Penkovskiy's suggestions for appropriate reactions to Soviet moves basically paralleled what actually happened. They were the basis for a special national intelligence estimate (SNIE) on 20 September 1961 that was passed to US decision makers as part of the planning process for US and Allied responses to Khrushchev's demands. Penkovskiy's reporting in September was the subject of another SNIE, 11-10/1-61, dated 5 October 1961. Whatever the actual effects of US and other western actions, in the end, Khrushchev did not order the access to West Berlin closed and the more serious military scenarios did not play out.

The whole episode gradually receded until Khrushchev was removed from power in 1964. In the meantime, his actions served to focus Western attention on the conventional military threat posed by the Warsaw Pact forces in Europe. In the USSR, the military began to raise questions about a doctrine dependent on massive nuclear-missile strikes. In a sense, the Soviets were a few years behind changes underway in the United States that were foreshadowed by General Maxwell Taylor's influential 1959 book, *The Uncertain Trumpet*.[27]

The seriousness of the confrontations notwithstanding, the Soviet military preparations and movements associated with the crisis provided Western intelligence valuable information about the organization and strength of the Warsaw Pact ground forces—Penkovskiy's reporting provided further understanding of the potential foe.

US Announced Responses to Khrushchev's Moves in Berlin

To demonstrate US intentions not to abandon Berlin, President Kennedy announced by radio and television on 25 July 1961 that his administration was beginning a program to enlarge the US Army and mobilize Reserve and National Guard forces to strengthen US forces in Europe and to send additional forces to West Berlin.

Deputy Secretary of Defense, Roswell Gilpatric, followed up the President's 25 September 1961 speech to the UN General Assembly by telling the US Business Council on 21 October 1961 that the United States not only would significantly improve its forces protecting Europe but would further augment them should the USSR pursue an aggressive course in Berlin.

---

[26] See the Catalogue of Documents, Chapter II, Document II-13 for the Penkovskiy report exposing Khrushchev's threats to use ICBMs as unfounded. [27] General Maxwell D. Taylor U.S.A. (Ret.), The Uncertain Trumpet (New York: Harper Bothers, Publishers, 1959).

Top: 1944: First Ukrainian Front; from right to left, Penkovskiy; Lieutenant General Varentsov; Pozovnyy, Adjutant to Varentsov; and an orderly.
Bottom: Graduating class of the Dzerzhinzkiy Artillery Engineering Academy; Penkovskiy is the third from right in the front row.

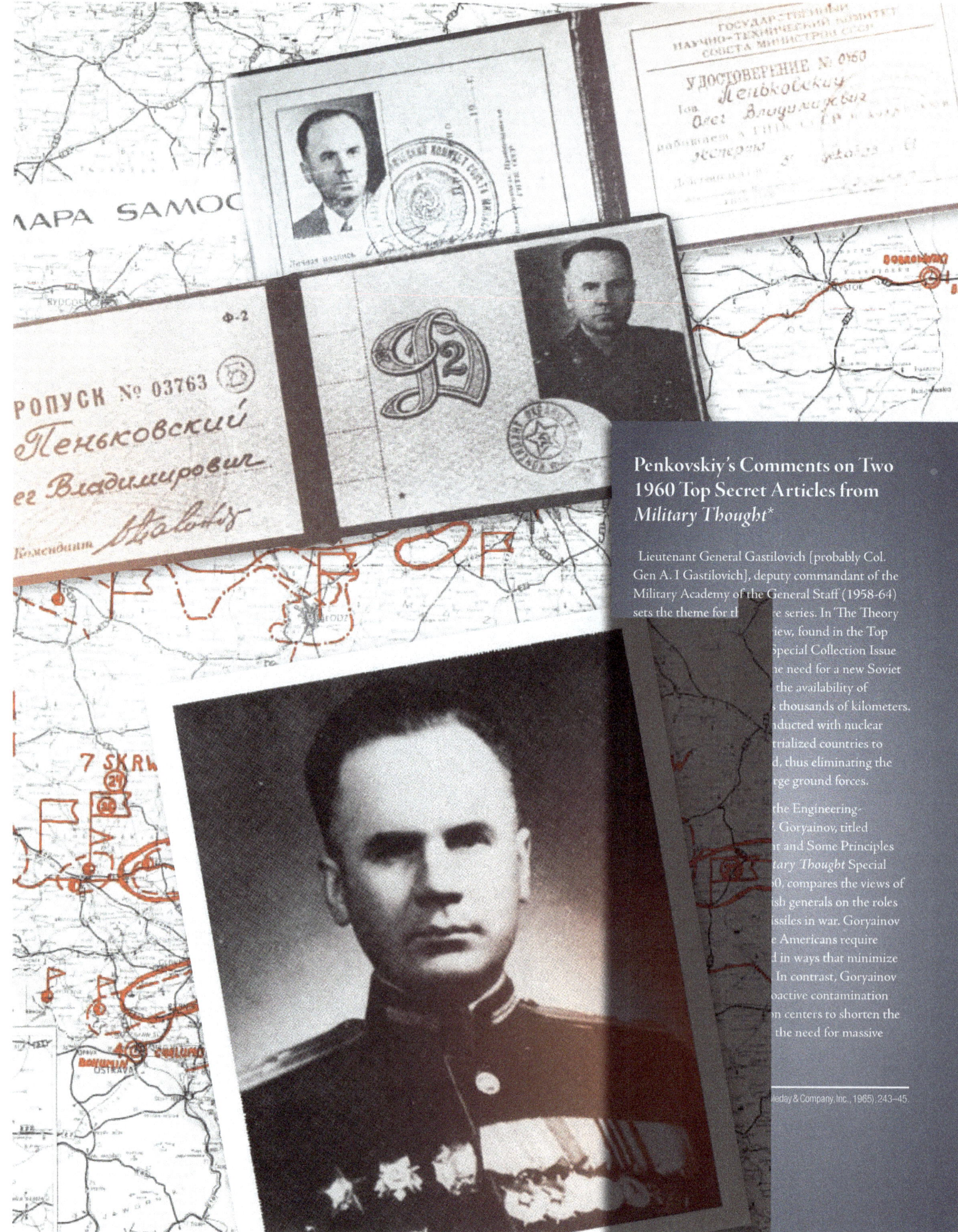

Penkovskiy's Comments on Two 1960 Top Secret Articles from *Military Thought**

Lieutenant General Gastilovich [probably Col. Gen A. I Gastilovich], deputy commandant of the Military Academy of the General Staff (1958-64) sets the theme for the entire series. In 'The Theory ... view, found in the Top ... Special Collection Issue ... the need for a new Soviet ... the availability of ... thousands of kilometers. ... ducted with nuclear ... trialized countries to ... d, thus eliminating the ... rge ground forces.

... the Engineering- ... Goryainov, titled ... t and Some Principles ... tary Thought* Special ... 60, compares the views of ... ish generals on the roles ... issiles in war. Goryainov ... e Americans require ... d in ways that minimize ... In contrast, Goryainov ... oactive contamination ... n centers to shorten the ... the need for massive

...leday & Company, Inc., 1965), 243–45.

CHAPTER III
Soviet Debate on Military Doctrine and Strategy: The Contribution of Col. Oleg Penkovskiy (1955–1964)

Stalin's death ended proscriptions against discussion of nuclear strategy. The Soviet military soon initiated a debate on military doctrine, a debate that centered on the effect of the rapidly advancing weapons technologies, especially the development of nuclear weapons and missile delivery systems. Early debate demonstrated a surprisingly unsophisticated appreciation of the impact of nuclear weapons by placing emphasis on adapting the new weapons to traditional battlefield concepts. As more and better weapons became available and their potency better understood, the focus shifted to modifying traditional concepts to suit contemporary trends in military science and art. By the end of the 1950s, the Soviets addressed the questions of whether all crises would require the use of nuclear weapons, would the conventional phase precede nuclear attacks, would conventional military means be useful in some crises, and whether antagonists could prevent limited wars from escalating to a general war.

USSR Developments and the Warsaw Pact

The historical prime mission of the Soviet military was the strategic defense of the homeland, focused on massive ground forces and supported by a clearly subordinate navy and air force. Soviet experience during World War II reinforced this concept of military mission.[28] After the elimination of German and Japanese military, the United States stood as the Soviets' principal source of opposition. To bring military power to bear against the United States, Stalin launched a major program to build medium and long range bombers and naval forces. He believed the basic nature of war would remain unchanged. US military analysts as early as 1947 assessed this belief would dominate Soviet military strategy. Until Stalin died in March 1953, his position effectively choked off theoretical discussion in the Soviet military press about integrating nuclear weapons into military doctrine.

As change swept through the Soviet hierarchy in 1953, the military must have seen that the time was ripe for throwing off Stalin's straightjacket on military thinking. The November 1953 issue of *Military Thought* contained an excellent illustration of the intellectual ferment. The editor urged contributors to attend to the times. "The military art of the Soviet Army must take into account a whole series of new phenomena which have arisen in the postwar period." By May 1954 the Ministry of Defense had enunciated a new doctrine addressing the role of nuclear weapons and missiles in its *Manual on the Characteristics of the Conduct of Combat Operations under Conditions of the Employment of Nuclear Weapons*. The Soviet military press undertook a systematic effort to inform military officers of the character, potential, and effect on the military of the new weapons and rapidly advancing weapon technologies, and to induce responsible officers to write about adapting the new weapons to traditional concepts of military science and military art. The debate continued throughout the 1950s.

During the latter 1950s, Khrushchev pursued a new military doctrine consistent with new weapon capabilities and his economic priorities. Articles appearing in the Soviet military press began to indicate a divergence in opinion among the military leadership about Soviet doctrine for the future. While their ground forces remained huge by US standards, the Soviets lagged in the production of both intercontinental-delivery systems and nuclear weapons, although their capabilities to make both were improving. No matter what was the actual cause behind the drive for a new military doctrine, Khrushchev and the Soviet military were certainly influenced by the implicit threat from the massive

---

28 The material in this section on history after WWII and into early 1950s is drawn from several sources. The main source of this information is contained in the Catalogue of Documents, Chapter III, Document III-5 "Historical Background Since World War II," Section I, *Soviet Naval Strategy and Its effect on the Development of Naval Forces 1953-63*, 22 October 1963, 23–30.

American nuclear forces, the accession of West Germany into NATO, and a West German rearmament program. During this period the Soviet military did reach an uneasy consensus on the place of nuclear weapons in its operational doctrine. The Field Services Regulations issued on 2 March 1959—and passed to the West by Penkovskiy in 1961—represented the culmination of the line of military thought evident after the death of Stalin. Almost as soon as it was published, however, it was overtaken by agitation for a dramatically new direction in military theory.

Seeing the potential of the nuclear arms as a cheap and flexible means of providing greater security and prominence for the USSR, Khrushchev outlined a new military policy in his report to the Supreme Soviet in January 1960. His plan in essence was to rely mainly on nuclear-missile forces, to reduce military manpower substantially, and to accelerate the retirement of older weapons. This, he asserted, was the force structure best suited both to advance Soviet political and economic interests, and to fight a war when necessary. Khrushchev's speech set off an impassioned debate among the Soviet military in open-source and classified publications.

In 1960 the Soviets began publishing a Top Secret "Special Collection" of *Military Thought*[29] that had limited distribution. It provided a forum for high-ranking military officers to debate the problems of fighting a future war in the context of forces equipped with a multitude of long-range nuclear weapons. Under Khrushchev's apparent tutelage, several well-placed Soviet general officers proposed a doctrine for conquering Europe that relied heavily on massive nuclear strikes. It assigned little role to conventional ground forces or to the Warsaw Pact allies except perhaps for air defense of the approaches to the Soviet Union. The more conservative elements of the military opposed much of this new thinking. These "traditionalists" began to question reliance on a military doctrine dependent almost solely on massive nuclear-missile strikes and instead posited the need for large armored forces as well. Beginning in 1961, Colonel Penkovskiy passed this series of classified articles to the West.

In addition to the *Military Thought* articles, Penkovskiy drew on his ties to some of the most senior officers in the Ministry of Defense and related organizations to supply priceless commentary about Soviet intentions, Soviet military leadership thinking on the character of war, Soviet and Warsaw Pact capabilities, and the organization of Warsaw Pact forces for war. He reported Soviet officers were concerned about the readiness of the military to face a confrontation with the United States and NATO that might result from Khrushchev's threats to sign a separate treaty with East Germany. He provided invaluable insight into Khrushchev's inclination to use a massive concentration of conventional weapons, especially tanks, in confrontations with the West, notwithstanding his championing

US Discussions

Following Dwight Eisenhower's inauguration in January 1953, his administration reviewed the US military and formulated a policy it called the New Look. This policy sought to deter communist aggression of any sort by threatening prompt nuclear reprisal. The resulting doctrine of massive retaliation focused on the delivery, by bombers and later by missiles, of hundreds, if not thousands, of nuclear weapons against an enemy. Accordingly, the United States sharply increased the size and capability of its nuclear armed air forces and drastically reduced resources allocated to US ground forces. It also accorded low priority in military doctrine and strategy to tactical air forces that did not deliver nuclear weapons.*
In 1961, however, the Kennedy administration shifted US doctrine toward a full spectrum of nonnuclear and nuclear capabilities, especially after the experience of the Berlin crisis.

---

* For more on this policy, see History of the Office of the Secretary of Defense, "Strategy, Money and the New Look, 1953-1956. Volume III, Richard M. Leighton, Historical Office of the Secretary of Defense, Washington, D.C. 20001.

of a doctrine that denigrated their significance. Penkovskiy presented the West with the Soviet idealized view of military doctrine as well as the practical consequence of contemporary Soviet reality. For example, he explained the Soviets had deployed no intercontinental ballistic missiles (ICBMs) in 1960 and 1961, despite statements implying they had massive numbers of intercontinental strike systems. Penkovskiy's information on Khrushchev's military contingency plan for the Berlin crisis illustrated again the gap between the new doctrinal positions and military realities in the early 1960s.

Intelligence Sources and Analysis

The efforts of CIA to understand the Soviet–Warsaw Pact forces increased steadily during this period, as Secretary of Defense McNamara and other officials of the Kennedy and Johnson administrations asked CIA to address a broader array of questions about Soviet military capabilities. Analysts from the DI's Office of Research and Reports (ORR) and the DI Research Staff in 1964 contributed to the first NIE devoted exclusively to Soviet and East European theater forces. CIA

---

[29] The Soviets continued to publish a secret edition of *Military Thought*.

CIA ANALYSIS OF THE WARSAW PACT FORCES: THE IMPORTANCE OF CLANDESTINE REPORTING

devoted more analytic resources to these issues, but not until 1967 did it establish the Office of Strategic Research (OSR) in the DI to focus on military analysis of the Soviet–Warsaw Pact forces, and other target military forces, capabilities, and intentions.

During the same period CIA and other IC analysts gained two new tools with which to develop estimates of Soviet military capabilities and intentions:

▸ Photography from the Corona satellite program supplied information on force locations and new developments with much greater accuracy than any previous system.

▸ Clandestine reporting by Colonel Penkovskiy provided the first high-level insight into the development of Soviet military hardware and strategy and a wealth of data about the military establishment.

Analysts now could determine how the Soviets envisioned their total force from intermediate-range ballistic missiles (IRBMs) to infantry and tank regiments would operate against NATO in Europe. Analysts began to understand, moreover, some of the discontinuities that characterized developments in the Soviet forces and as they were implied by Soviet military doctrine.

Penkovskiy's clandestine reporting remained relevant long after the KGB apprehended him in 1962 because much of it represented the discussion by senior officers of major issues in Soviet military thinking for the future development of weapons and strategy. For more than 10 years, the IC continued to base analyses on his reporting about Warsaw Pact plans, capabilities and intentions about developments in Soviet strategic thought, even as other, more circumstantial evidence became available. When key East European clandestine sources began supplying information in the late 1960s and early 1970s, the Penkovskiy collection helped validate the relevance of the new evidence for evaluating the Warsaw Pact, proving the enduring value of the work of this remarkable Russian.

Documents written by Marshal of the Soviet Union R. Ya. Malinovskiy, obtained for the United States by Oleg Penkovskiy.

```
COUNTRY           :   USSR
SUBJECT           :   MILITARY THOUGHT (TOP SECRET):
                      "Some Thoughts on the Development
                      of the Soviet Army Tank Troops",
                      by Marshal of the Soviet Union
                      R. Malinovskiy
DATE OF INFO      :   December 1961
APPRAISAL OF
CONTENT           :   Documentary
SOURCE            :   A reliable source (B).
```

Following is a verbatim translation of an article titled "Some Thoughts on the Development of the Soviet Army Tank Troops", by Marshal of the Soviet Union R. Malinovskiy.

	USSR T-55 with D-10T2s gun	T-62	USA M48A2	M-60	Britain "Centurion" MK-IX-X
Year produced	1958	1961	1956	1960	1959
Combat weight, tons	36	36.5	46	46.27	51
Armor protection in mm: hull-front	100	100	110	About 150	76
side	80	80	51–76	51–76	51
turret – front	200	200	178	178	152
Armament (caliber in mm)	100	115	90	105	105
Muzzle velocity of armor-piercing shell, m/sec	895	1615	930 / 1245 (subcaliber)	1475 (subcaliber)	1475
Armor penetration in mm at 2000 m with an angle of fire of 0° to 60°: armor-piercing shell	122–55	—	130–45	—	—
subcaliber shell	Being developed	270–100	200–60	220–85	220–85
shaped charge antitank shell	390–150	440–200	—	—	—
Unit of fire	43	40	60	57	70
Maximum speed, kph	50	48	45	48	34
Horsepower of engine	580	580	850	750	650
Cruising range, km	500	500	310	400	190

Cold War International History Project
Virtual Archive

Collection: Cuban Missile Crisis

List of Troops and Commanders to take part in Operation "Anadyr."

Source:

Date:
06/20/1962

Description:
A description of the staff and crew of the Soviet Operation "Anadyr."

Top Secret
Special Importance
In One Copy

Diagram
Of the Organization of the Group of Soviet Forces for "Anadyr"

Commander of the
Group of Soviet Forces
General of the Army I.A. Pliyev

Staff Deputies
(133 pers.)
Lt. Gen. V.V. Akhindinov First-Deputy—Lt. Gen.
Sections Of Av. P.B. Dankevich
Operational Directorate For Naval Affairs--Vice
(22 pers.) Adm. G.S. Abashvili
For Air Defense—Lt.
Col. N.A. Ivanov
Intelligence Gen Av. S.N. Grechko
(11 pers.) For the Air Forces--Col.
Communications Gen. Av. V.I. Davidkov
(11 pers.) For Special (nuclear)
Ballistics Armaments—[blank]
(6 pers.) For Combat Training—
Cartographic and Geodosy Maj. Gen. L.S. Garbuz
(9 pers.) For the Rear Services--
Meteorological Service Maj. Gen.N.R. Pilipenko
(8 pers.) Deputy—Maj. Gen.
Sixth Section [unidentified] Tech. Trps. A.A. (4 pers.) Dement'ev
Personnel and Records
(7 pers.)
Eighth Section [unidentified]
(13 pers.)

Missile Forces (RV)
43rd Missile Division
665th Missile Regiment (R-14 with PRTB)
668th Missile Regiment (R-14 with PRTB)
79th Missile Regiment (R-12 with PRTB)
181st Missile Regiment (R-12 with PRTB)
664th Missile Regiment (R-12 with PRTB)
(Eight launchers per regiment)

Air Defense Forces (PVO)
11th Antiaircraft Division
16th Antiaircraft Regiment
276th Antiaircraft Regiment
500th Antiaircraft Regiment [Trans: 6 launchers in each battalion]
4 battalions in each AA Regiment
Separate Radar Battalion 10th Antiaircraft Division
294th Antiaircraft Regiment
318th Antiaircraft Regiment
466th Antiaircraft Regiment
32nd Fighter Aviation Regiment
40 MiG-21s
Separate Radar Battalion

Air Forces (VVS)
561st FKR (Frontal Cruise Missile) Regiment
584th FKR Regiment
Each regiment with 8 launchers and PRTB
437th Separate Helicopter Regiment
33 Mi-4 helicopters
134 Separate Aviation Communications Squadron 11 aircraft

Ground Forces (SV)
302nd Separate Motorized Rifle Regiment
314th Separate Motorized Rifle Regiment
400th Separate Motorized Rifle Regiment
496th Separate Motorized Rifle Regiment

Naval Forces (VMF)
Submarine Squadron
18th Missile Submarine Division
7 submarines
211th Submarine Brigade
4 submarines
Two submarine tenders (floating support bases)
Surface Ship Squadron
2 cruisers, 2 missile destroyers, 2 destroyers
Missile Patrol Boat Brigade
12 missile patrol boats (cutters)
Sopka Missile Regiment [coastal defense cruise missile]
6 launchers
Aviation Mine-Torpedo Regiment
33 IL-28 aircraft
[Trans: Includes 3 trainers]
Detachment of Support Ships
2 tankers
2 dry cargo ships
1 floating repair ship

Rear Services
Field Bakery Factory
Hospitals (3 at 200 beds each)
Sanitary-antiepidemiological detachment
Company to service entry to the bases
Food storage stocks (2)
Warehouse
Missile and aviation fuel stations (2)
Fuel oil for the Navy (2)

Chief of the Main Operations Directorate of the General Staff
Colonel General S.P. Ivanov [signature]
20 June 1962

From Cold War International History Project, CWIHP.org, used with permission.

CHAPTER IV
New Insights into the Warsaw Pact Forces and Doctrine – The Cuban Missile Crisis (1962)

This chapter highlights the importance of the clandestine reporting before and during the Cuban Missile Crisis, the relationship of the reporting to the general NATO–Warsaw Pact equation, and the impact of analytic experience gained during the crisis in evaluating the reporting.

Khrushchev's Gamble Provides an Intelligence Bonanza

After the failure of his Berlin gambit and with the US advantage in intercontinental attack capabilities growing, Khrushchev in a break with precedent launched the first major expeditionary force outside the Soviet orbit since WWII. The Soviet plans in May 1962 called for the deploying to Cuba a large number of strategic-range guided missiles with an integrated military force to protect them.[30]

In their discussions of Soviet military doctrine in 1960–61, the Soviets hotly contested the role of medium-range ballistic missiles (MRBMs) and IRBMs in Soviet strategy and operations against NATO. Most participants in the internal high-level military debates posited the decisive importance of having those missiles to destroy the enemy's nuclear weapons located deep in the theater, beyond the range of tactical aviation. They argued for leaving the destruction of US-based nuclear delivery systems to the ICBMs and long-range bombers of the Supreme High Command. Some protagonists insisted that the nuclear forces, especially MRBMS and IRBMs, could defeat NATO without much assistance from the ground forces beyond some minor mopping up and occupation tasks. By early 1962, the principals seemed to be reaching a consensus that combining missile and conventional land forces was the correct operational solution.

The mix of forces involved in Khrushchev's Cuban adventure—missile, ground, air, air defense, coastal defense, and naval—generally copied those deployed against NATO. Indeed, the specific forces sent to Cuba came from larger groupings in the western USSR, whose contingent mission had been the destruction of NATO in Europe. The special Top Secret series of *Military Thought* described various proposals to integrate long-range missiles into theater war planning and utilize the shorter range nuclear-armed rockets known as FROGs that were deployed with the Soviet and other Warsaw Pact ground armies in Europe. The composition of the Soviet Group of Forces sent to Cuba reflected real preferences of the military leadership when confronted with an unrehearsed potential combat situation.

The deployment to Cuba of a virtual cross section of these forces provided military intelligence analysts, for the first time, an important example of what Soviet forces looked like when they were out of garrison and away from the supporting infrastructure of their Warsaw Pact Allies. It also allowed analysts to factor out other confusing aspects of military operations like mobilization.

Intelligence Sources and Analysis

Not evident in contemporary intelligence publications because of its sensitivity was the real contribution of Col. Oleg Penkovskiy. Even though he was unable to provide any information about the actual Soviet deployment of forces to Cuba, he had already delivered technical specifications and detailed operational information on the types of missiles that the USSR sent in the fall of 1962. Penkovskiy had managed to photograph and pass highly sensitive documents that proved invaluable during the crisis. They were the source for most of the understanding analysts had of field

---

30 See Mary S McAuliffe, ed., *Cuban Missile Crisis 1962* (Washington, DC: Center for the Study of Intelligence, 1992) for many of the intelligence documents issued during the crisis period as well as a sample of the clandestine reporting from the CIA's Cuban sources. This study is available on CIA's website, www.cia.gov. **31** FROG is the acronym for "Free Rocket over Ground," the name for large unguided missiles.

deployment and standard operating procedures for missile forces, the time required to achieve different levels of readiness, and the camouflage the Soviets prescribed to hide their forces, all of which contributed to US response decisions during the Cuban Missile Crisis.

Other information from Penkovskiy provided the basis for the analytical judgments that allowed the United States to calculate reaction times, capabilities, and limitations of the deployed Soviet air defense missile systems. The descriptions and the technical specifications of the "V-75" or SA-2, a surface-to-air missile, and the discussions in the Top Secret 1960–61 special collection *Military Thought* series about the limitations of the SA-2 and the overall air defense organization disclosed critical Soviet vulnerabilities to high-speed low-level air attack. This information enabled US tactical reconnaissance planes to fly frequently over Cuba and monitor the status of Soviet missile deployments and other militarily important targets without the loss of a single low flying reconnaissance aircraft. This information would have been even more critical had the United States implemented plans calling for more than 500 sorties in the first day for the neutralization or destruction of Soviet missiles, the invasion of Cuba, and the destruction or capture of the Soviet ground and air forces deployed there.[32] After Khrushchev agreed to remove the missiles and light bombers from Cuba, analysts relied on imagery, clandestine reporting, and information from Cuban immigrants to verify that no MRBMs remained and the agreement was met.[33]

In addition to the *Military Thought* articles, Penkovskiy supplied invaluable commentary about general Soviet intentions, the Soviet military leadership's thoughts about the nature of war, Soviet and Warsaw Pact military capabilities, and the organization of the Warsaw Pact forces for war. All of this contributed to Kennedy's confidence in the judgments reached by the intelligence analysts.

Although Penkovskiy talked earlier with US intelligence officers about Soviet military aid to Cuba following the April 1961 Bay of Pigs disaster, he was unable to warn or give any details of the buildup of forces in Cuba. Clandestine sources in Cuba, however, supplied enough timely information about developments on the ground to prompt the United States to launch the U-2 reconnaissance flights that yielded detailed, incontrovertible evidence of the Soviet deployment.

In sum, there were three major types of human intelligence sources during the Cuban Missile Crisis.

➤ **The inside source**, Colonel Oleg Penkovskiy, who provided Soviet classified documents that greatly helped military analysts understand how the Soviets set up and conducted missile operations.

➤ **Cuban refugees**, who described being displaced from their farms, and thus furnished clues about where Soviet deployed the missiles.

➤ **Clandestine sources inside Cuba**, who delivered information that cued US flight plans for reconnaissance aircraft.

Cuban Missile Crisis, 1962
SA-2 Air Defense Missiles

---

[32] See FRUS 1961-1963 Volume XI, p. 267, The Cuban Missile Crisis and Aftermath, Department of State, Washington, DC, 1996. [33] Ibid.

U-2 Overflights of Cuba, October 1962

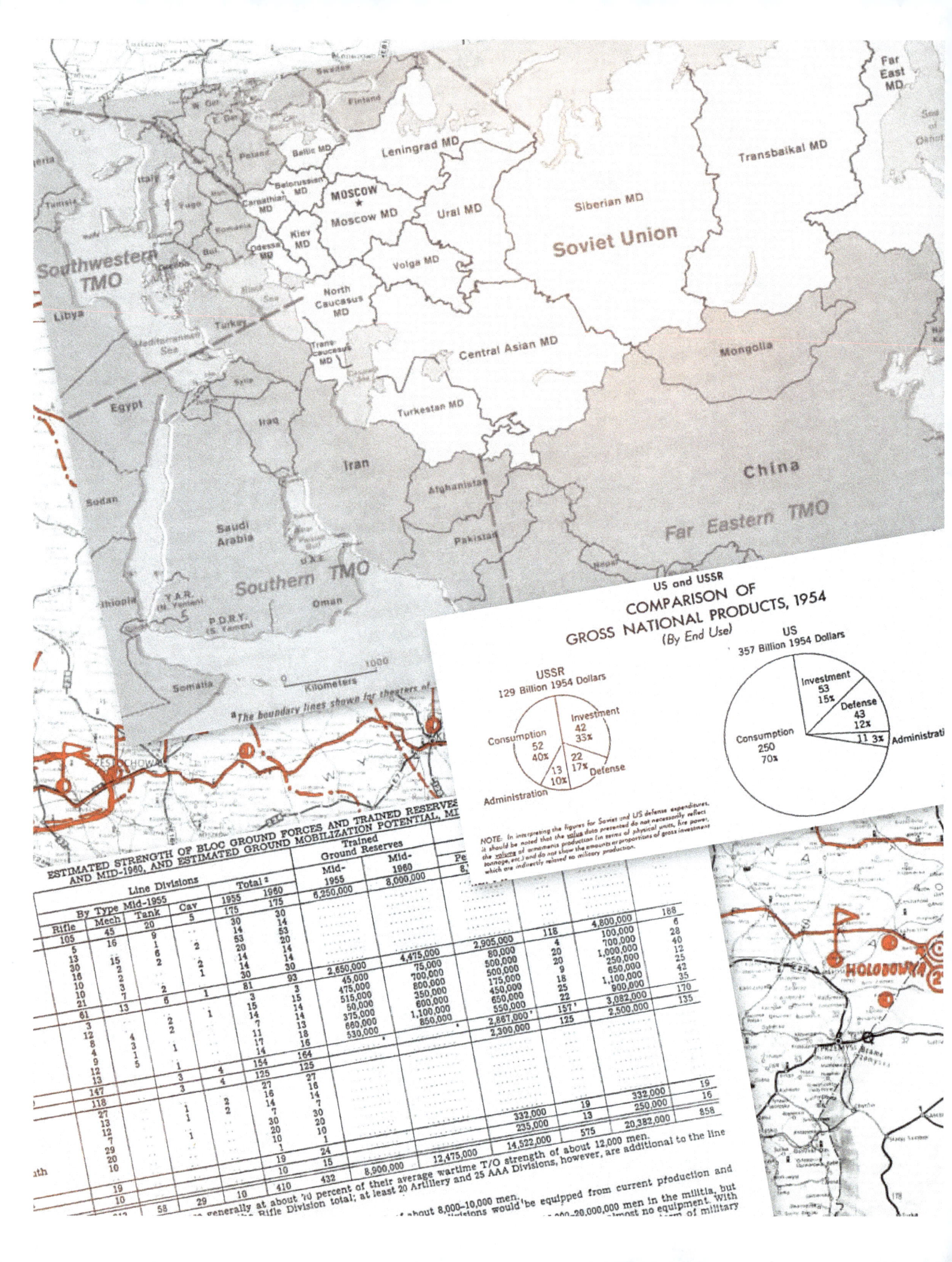

CHAPTER V

New Estimates of the Soviet Ground Forces (1963–1968)

In early 1963, Secretary of Defense McNamara wrote DCI John McCone to convey his concern that US national intelligence estimates about Soviet forces and capabilities[34] were "causing NATO Allies and many Americans to despair of the possibility of achieving adequate non-nuclear forces." The Secretary of Defense stated that he believed "the estimates of the strength of the Soviet ground forces…contained in NIE 11-14-62 were overstated." Referring to the NIE, he wrote that he "could not understand how the Soviets, with the resources available to them, could have the number of 'well-trained divisions equipped with the excellent materiel' that the IC was estimating they had, when the United States could not afford even half that number of forces." McNamara requested the DCI and the Director of the Defense Intelligence Agency (D/DIA) to reexamine the estimates. In the spring of 1963, a team of CIA and DIA intelligence analysts was formed to address these concerns and to produce a joint study.

Defining the Problem

According to the officer in charge of the CIA effort, Dr. Edward Proctor, estimating the size and capabilities of Soviet forces in general posed problems; a Soviet division, for example, was not like a US division.[35] Analysts had assessed the ground forces on the basis of captured Soviet documents, observations and statements by defectors, and bits and pieces of additional information. They had little opportunity to confirm the continued existence of many of the units known in the time of Stalin.

The 1962 estimate,[36] based on the contributions of the US Army and the new DIA, had described a Soviet force of some 80 combat-ready divisions, with an additional 65 divisions "requiring substantial augmentation before commitment to combat." It also calculated that, given 30 days to mobilize before hostilities began, the Soviets could expand their total forces to about 100 combat-ready divisions and 125 others less well prepared. Earlier estimates had calculated a Soviet Army of 175 active divisions and an additional 125 available in 30 days.[37] It is no wonder the Secretary of Defense wanted a better appraisal. The joint team of CIA and DIA analysts was instructed to discard all past positions and to start from scratch to determine the number of divisions the Soviets actually had in 1962. New intelligence from Penkovskiy and satellite photography[38] made possible a critical review and revision of the previous estimates.

Revising the Estimates of the Strength of Soviet–Warsaw Pact Forces

By the time the Secretary of Defense made his request for a new study, the analysts had accumulated much information about Soviet ground forces:

- The reductions[39] and reorganizations in the 1950s provided insight into the modifications of the organization of the combat divisions of the ground forces to about 1960.

- Information from Popov, Penkovskiy, and other sources of military writings provided insights into the changes in the ground forces on an aggregate level.

- The 1961 Berlin and 1962 Cuban crises provided additional insights into the organization, size and operational planning for the Warsaw Pact Ground Forces.

---

[34] Ibid. Catalogue of Documents, Chapter V, Document V-13. p 3, reported that Soviet ground forces were defined to include "those Soviet military personnel performing functions similar to most of those performed by the US Army with the principal exception of continental air defenses." [35] Edward Proctor interview with John Bird, 22 April 2008. [36] See Catalogue of Documents, Chapter V, Document V-8a for the 1962 NIE 11-14-62, Capabilities of Soviet Theater Forces. [37] See Catalogue of Documents, Chapter I, Document I-78, NIE 11-4-58, page 43. [38] Low-resolution satellite photography began covering military installations in 1960. [39] See Catalogue of Documents, Chapter VI, Document VI-7, page 4, Caesar XXVI, Warsaw Pact Military Strategy: *A Compromise in Soviet Strategic Thinking*, for a summary of various Soviet announcements of reductions in forces and reassignments from the Warsaw Pact countries during the period 1958–65.

Nonetheless, determining the details of the changes unit by unit had still been beyond what the evidence would bear. Moreover, because of the lack of specific information about the Soviet reorganizations of the early 1960s, analysts were less certain about current organizational standards. In the words of the authors of the Joint CIA-DIA Panel Study in 1963: "In the mid-1950s good insights into divisional and other TO&Es [tables of organization and equipment] were obtained from clandestine and documentary sources. Thus far, information of similar quality is not available for the TO&Es of divisions reorganized since the 1960s."[40]

The Joint Study authors described the problem they needed to address and the process they devised to accomplish the assessments as they saw them at the time:

> *"For the assessment of the personnel strength of the Soviet ground forces by unit or in the aggregate there is no unique type of intelligence source that has as yet become available. The process is one of gathering fragmentary bits of information in print from which inferences can be drawn with varying degrees of confidence. In general, the statements that are made regarding the quality of each source of information are applicable to questions of Soviet personnel strengths. Attachés and military liaison officers can gain general appreciations of manning levels at the various installations they observe, but the presence of reservists in training or the co-location of units usually obscures the meaningfulness of such appreciations. In East Germany approximate head counts could be made for small units when such units were en route as units. Similarly, defectors and repatriates, covert sources and informants can provide reasonably trustworthy indications with respect to the small units in which they have served. However, more broadly knowledgeable sources had been rare."[41]*

The satellite photographic coverage of the whole USSR made it possible for the first time to ascertain the existence of most of the division sized units in 1963. Questions did remain, however, because of the rudimentary quality typical of the early satellite photography.

In the Second Panel Report—on Soviet Ground forces—completed in 1965, the authors noted that for assessing production and inventory of land armaments:

> *The collective output from [all] sources [to 1963] has proved disappointing in quality, timeliness and comprehensiveness. In addition none of the sources has provided consistent coverage over the period since World War II. This situation is not surprising in view of the nature of the problem.*
>
> *Land combat equipment and ammunition represent a wide variety of comparatively small items. Production can be dispersed widely in a number of different types of plants. Storage can be accomplished in a variety of ways with little difficulty. Different models may appear identical to all but trained observers.*

Even Penkovskiy, with his access in the highest levels in the Ministry of Defense, was unable to provide information on the rates of production or inventories of land armaments.

The CIA/DIA team analyzed each division of ground forces by combining Penkovskiy's information on the Soviet theory of mobilization and peacetime readiness of forces with newly available satellite photography. Even though the satellite photos were of poor quality for this task, the classified Soviet military documents supplied by Penkovskiy and the evidence provided by other human sources enabled the estimative process to proceed.

The Joint Study concluded that:

➢ With a high degree of confidence between 115–135 Soviet ground forces divisions, including 22–45 cadre (skeleton) divisions existed in the first half of 1963.

➢ The total number could be as low as 100 or as high as 150.

➢ The cadre divisions had few troops but could be fleshed out with reservists in order to participate in a subsequent stage of the war.

The study found no basis for the 125 additional divisions to be mobilized in 30 days mentioned in earlier estimates. Clearly, however, the Soviet army was larger in many respects than the ground forces of NATO but significantly smaller than the analysts previously thought. Unanswered questions about the quality of those forces remained. Nonetheless, the doctrinal discussions in the documents Penkovskiy passed to the West put the seemingly confusing picture of the whole ground forces' establishment into meaningful perspective.

40 This refers to the TO&Es Popov provided in the mid-1950, see Catalogue of Documents, Chapter I, Documents I-15, I-67, I-68, I-69, I-70, I-71, I-72. **41** Ibid. Catalogue of Documents, Chapter V, Document V-13, page 55.

*Clarifying the Estimate of Capabilities
and Mobilization of Soviet–Warsaw Pact Forces*

After addressing the questions about the quantity of forces, the next all-source analytic challenge was to understand the qualitative distinctions between theory and practice. Secretary McNamara again requested a CIA-DIA team of analysts be brought together. Throughout 1967 and 1968, this team sought better estimates of the capabilities of the Warsaw Pact to mobilize forces and strengthen the area opposite NATO in the central region of Europe. The important question was how well the Soviets could carry out the intentions described in their writings—specifically, how well the divisions were manned and equipped and how well the rear echelons could transport and supply war materiel to combat units in order to meet Soviet requirements for a war with NATO.

Studying the 1962 Soviet expedition to Cuba increased the confidence of military analysts in estimates of what a full regiment might look like. Soviet Ministry of Defense classified documents, such as the 1959 *Field Service Regulations of the Armed Forces of the USSR* and the 1962 draft of the revised version, informed them on how the forces generally would be used. Pieces of evidence about the process of mobilization and reinforcement, found within numerous Soviet classified documents copied by Penkovskiy, provided an increasingly clear picture of the Soviet forces aimed at NATO. Nonetheless, it was also clear that the observations and other evidence of Soviet military units suggested a gap between what the theoretical journals described and the actual condition of typical Soviet units on the ground.

The analysis improved significantly once high resolution imagery from KH-7 satellites became available during the period 1965–68. Analysts combined this information with the evidence from human sources, reconstructed their view of the organization of the Soviet divisions, and judged their actual size and readiness. There were, of course, many more ingredients involved in the all-source analysis, but the synergistic effects of the documentary and other human source evidence with the new higher resolution imagery of the KH-7 system constituted the basis of major improvements in the analysis of Warsaw Pact ground forces. These improvements were evident in the marked differences, for example, between the contributions to NIE 11-14-67 and NIE 11-14-68. The latter estimate contained a much more detailed assessment of the forces, including their overall size and intended use in operations against the West, than had existed since the end of WWII.

By 1969 the CIA assessed that military analysis during the 1960s had made strides in understanding Soviet capabilities for conducting a war against NATO in the Central Region, but it had not answered all of Secretary McNamara's questions:

> *Major areas of uncertainty about the capabilities of the Soviet ground forces remain. The most significant gap is in the understanding of service-support organization and capabilities above the level of the division. The detailed study of Soviet logistical capabilities requires different methodologies than have been applied to the study of the combat forces, and depends to a greater degree on sources of information other than overhead photography. Considerable uncertainty also remains about the peacetime personnel strengths of combat support units inside the USSR.[42]*

The two studies, however, had not addressed the Soviet plan for conducting a war with NATO in the Central Region of Europe. That study did not occur until June 1968.

Warsaw pact general purpose forces available for early commitment in central Europe. From NIE 11-14-69 Soviet and East European General Purpose Force. 4 December 1969.

	Armies				Estimated Wartime Strength			
							AIRCRAFT	
CURRENTLY AVAILABLE FORCES	COMBINED ARMS	TANK	TACTICAL AIR	DIVISIONS	MEN	TANKS	GROUND ATTACK AND RECONNAISSANCE [a]	AIR DEFENSE [b]
GSFG and East German Army	5	2	1	26	405,000	6,500	400	640
Czechoslovak *Front*	3		1	12 [c]	180,000	3,000	260	300
Carpathian *Front* [d]	2–3	1	1	15	230,000	3,400	210	200
Polish *Front*	3		1	15 [e]	215,000	2,800	260	620
Northern Group of Forces in Poland			1	2	35,000	600	170	110
Belorussian *Front*	1	2	1	11 [f]	165,000	2,800	150	110
Baltic MD	1		1	5 [f]	60,000	1,000	200	70
TOTAL	15–16	5	7	86	1,290,000	20,100	1,650	2,050

[42] See Catalogue of Documents, Chapter V, Document V-61. Warsaw Pact Ground Forces Facing NATO, CIA/DI/OSR Intelligence Report, September 1969.

CHAPTER VI

Turmoil in the Soviet Sphere (1962–1968)

The Demise of Khrushchev

The Soviet Communist Party expelled Khrushchev from office in October 1964. During his last two years in power, many of his policies were halted or reversed. His tactics during the Berlin crisis had failed to bring about control of West Berlin, and he had to abandon his proposal for a separate peace treaty with East Germany.[43] Worse, the Berlin crisis drew the NATO countries closer together and motivated the Western alliance to improve its defenses. Khrushchev's Cuban gamble, moreover, ended in retreat when the United States forced him to remove the missiles. These failures humiliated him and the other Soviet leaders and exposed Soviet strategic inferiority to the world. The hangover from the two debacles would affect Soviet political and military policies well into the following decades.

In the aftermath of the two crises many of Khrushchev's foreign policy goals tied to the German question obstructed his desire to improve East-West relations, including favorable stability in Europe. Although the USSR concluded the Limited Test Ban Treaty with the United States and the United Kingdom in 1963, further efforts to manage the race in strategic weapons and ground forces and to obtain nonaggression agreements stalled. Had he achieved these goals, Khrushchev could have pressed forward with economic, agricultural, and resource allocation reforms at home and could have perceived opportunities to influence political changes in Western Europe to Soviet advantage, including the USSR's relationship with West Germany.

During the same period, fallout from the Sino-Soviet dispute caused Khrushchev political problems in Europe and military problems along the border with China. China initiated a propaganda and diplomatic campaign in Europe that used Khrushchev's plan to visit West Germany as evidence of Soviet intent to "sell out" East Germany in favor of West Germany. China also made claims to some Soviet territory, prompting Soviet military concern about the need to move troops there from Europe. The latter threat had implications for Khrushchev's goals to reduce Soviet forces and reallocate resources. Khrushchev seemed to calculate that the need to maintain forces in Europe and also along the Sino-Soviet border would prevent him from shifting resources to the nonmilitary sector. All of which added urgency to achieving his objectives in Europe.

Internal Warsaw Pact issues also plagued the Soviets. Albania severed diplomatic relations with the USSR in December 1961 and expelled Soviet naval ships from the base they occupied. Romania began to take a separate road on foreign policy, especially with West Germany, culminating in its recognition of the Federal Republic of Germany two months after Khrushchev's ouster. East Germany feared that rapprochement between West Germany and Moscow would weaken the position of Moscow on consolidating the status quo in Germany. Bonn made overtures to the Soviet Union for recognition, but clandestine reports indicated that, before dismissing Khrushchev, the Politburo cancelled a plan for him to visit Bonn.

According to CIA analysis at the time, in addition to the continuing repercussions from his failed policies on Berlin and Cuba, the many reported charges against Khrushchev at his "trial" by the CPSU Central Committee included his personal mishandling of the Sino-Soviet dispute, the total failure of his agriculture polices, and the fostering of a personality cult. The analysis also indicated that an immediate reason for Khrushchev's ouster was the fallout from his continued mishandling of German affairs during the period 1963 and 1964 and the plans he had for a plenum he had called for November 1964. Despite his removal, however, Soviet–West German policy, problems with East European allies, and internal problems raised during the final two years of Khrushchev's tenure did not change fundamentally until later in the decade.

---

[43] The treaty was ratified in September 1964. Moscow had settled for a Friendship and Mutual Assistance Treaty as a panacea for East Germany in place of the unattainable Peace Treaty in June 1964, about four months prior to Khrushchev's ouster. The treaty was ratified in September 1964.

The Brezhnev-Kosygin Team

Following the selection of Brezhnev as general secretary and Kosygin as premier to succeed Khrushchev in 1964, CIA analysts characterized the new "collective" leadership as cautious and conservative, one consumed by internal debates and political maneuvering to consolidate their positions. Astutely and in contrast to his predecessor, Brezhnev relied on the military for advice on strategic defense policy issues. His policies emphasized persistent international dangers, such as the 1966 US military expansion in Vietnam. He backed the military on the utility of conventional forces and supported increasing the strategic forces. He defended the interests of the military by buttressing investment in heavy industry and the defense sector of the Soviet economy. In contrast, apparently out of optimism on long-term international trends, Kosygin pursued policies that the military leadership opposed. He supported arms control talks, increased trade with the West, and more investment in agriculture and non-military industry.

Managing the Warsaw Pact

In 1966, Brezhnev moved to reorganize the military of the Warsaw Pact by focusing on the 1955 Statute of Unified Command and the creation of new military institutions. The NSWP members, however, had resisted agreeing to the full set of statutes because they granted the Soviets virtual control over the NSWP forces.

The Political Consultative Committee (PCC) of the Warsaw Pact continued to work on the Statutes to the Warsaw Pact Treaty. At a meeting in Budapest in March 1969, all member states except Romania adopted four statutes. The statutes established the Unified Armed Forces and Unified Command of the Warsaw Pact for Peace Time, the Committee of Defense Ministers, the Military Council, and the Unified Air Defense System, as well as the Staff and Technical Committee of the Combined Armed Forces. However, the members failed to agree on a Statute of Unified Command of the Warsaw Pact for War Time and did not announce the content or implementation of the statutes. In the mid-1970s, a well-placed clandestine source provided information about the content, approval, and ratification of the statutes.

The Soviets' difficulties with managing their Warsaw Pact allies notwithstanding, by the end of the 1960s CIA analysts retrospectively assessed that Brezhnev could look at the foreign policy of his first years as a success. The Soviet leadership kept large, well-equipped forces in Czechoslovakia, Poland, and East Germany. It also maintained its alliance with the East Europeans, whose territories and forces buffered the Soviet Union from NATO. Both achievements protected Soviet vital interests.

Intelligence Sources and Analysis

The early years of the Brezhnev-Kosygin regime coincided with one of the driest periods for clandestinely obtained Soviet military information. From Penkovskiy's apprehension in 1962 until the Soviet-Warsaw Pact invasion of Czechoslovakia in 1968, the IC lacked any important clandestine sources of Soviet military information. As events unfolded, some classified Soviet military documents from Penkovskiy that indicated doctrinal changes provided the basis for understanding the rationale for changes in doctrine and forces revealed in the open press and by other intelligence sources. For example, satellite photography supplied information about the quantity and quality of Soviet forces that was consistent with Penkovskiy's reporting and ultimately improved the IC's military estimates.

Even so, intelligence collection and analysis during the 1960s suffered from a number of shortcomings. The IC did not know at the beginning of the decade how the Soviets would conduct war with the West, how well they were prepared for such a war, how well their divisions were manned and equipped, how well their rear services transportation capabilities matched wartime requirements, and how well their supplies of war materiel matched their perceptions of the requirements of war with NATO. Moreover, while the Penkovskiy documents provided significant insights into Soviet thinking about operations and mobilization, they neither revealed contingency plans for war with NATO nor supplied a sufficient guide for the changes in the military organization and planning of the Warsaw Pact coincident with Brezhnev's initiatives.

Other clandestine information, however, did corroborate circumstantial or less comprehensive information about the organization and operation of forces in the war planning of the Warsaw Pact. The new information greatly clarified, for example, the changed roles of NSWP forces in these plans. Finished intelligence produced in 1968 was based on this information. Still, the Penkovskiy documents provided the broader theoretical basis for extrapolating from a basic war plan of the Warsaw Pact against NATO to conditions different from those assumed in that plan. When the Czech crisis was peaking in August 1968, analytical breakthroughs at the time and some excellent analysis and material from FBIS laid the foundation for concluding that the Soviets were preparing a force to invade Czechoslovakia that was larger than any amassed theretofore in peacetime. The Soviet and other Warsaw Pact nations' gross violation of Czech sovereignty followed.

After the invasion of Czechoslovakia, excellent military sources virtually flooded out of Warsaw Pact countries, and the CIA clandestine service recruited many of them. Dissatisfaction with the communist regimes controlling the Pact countries inspired these sources to work for the West. Some were extraordinarily

CIA ANALYSIS OF THE WARSAW PACT FORCES: THE IMPORTANCE OF CLANDESTINE REPORTING

well placed. The most important was Col. Ryszard Kuklinski of the Polish General Staff, who began his plans to work with the United States at about this time and ultimately established contact in 1972. Kuklinski and other sources provided information on the Warsaw Pact that corroborated and expanded upon Penkovskiy's reporting. The new information, when combined with Western observations of the Group of Soviet Forces in East Germany (GSFG) and the more theoretical and predictive military discussions in special editions of Military Thought between 1960 and 1962, allowed analysts to extrapolate from the documentary materials of the early 1960s to the status of the Warsaw Pact forces and doctrine in late 1960s and beyond.

Key Statements on Sovereignty and Communist Independence*

Soviet-Yugoslav Declaration (Pravda, 3 June 1955) "The two governments decided to proceed from the following principles: Respect for sovereignty, independence, integrity, and equality among states in mutual relations and relations with other countries… Adherence to the principle of mutual respect and noninterference in internal affairs for any reason whatsoever, be it for economic, political, or ideological nature, since questions of international order, of different social systems, and different forms of development of socialism are the exclusive business of the peoples of the respective countries.

General Secretary Brezhnev (Pravda, 13 November 1968): It is known, comrades, that there are common laws governing socialist construction, a deviation from which might lead to a deviation from socialism as such. And when the internal and external forces hostile to socialism seek to reverse the development of any socialist country toward the restoration of the capitalist order, when a threat to the cause of socialism in that country emerges, a threat to the security of the socialist community as a whole exists; this is no longer a problem of the people of that country but also a common problem, a concern for all socialist states.

It goes without saying that such an action as military aid to a fraternal country to cut short a threat to the socialist order is an extraordinary enforced step; it can be sparked off only by direct actions of the enemies of socialism inside the country and beyond its boundaries, actions creating a threat to the common interest of the camp of socialism.

Soviet-Yugoslav Joint Declarations (Pravda, 19 March 1988): "The USSR and SFRY underscore the historical role and abiding value of the universal principles contained in the Belgrade (1955) and Moscow (1956) declarations, and in particular: mutual respect for independence, sovereignty, and territorial integrity, equality, and impermissibility of interference in internal affairs under any pretext whatever…

"The USSR and SFRY confirm their commitment to the policy of peace and independence of peoples and countries, to their equal rights and the equal security of all countries irrespective of their size and potential, sociopolitical system. The ideas by which they are guided and the forms and character of their associations with other states, or their geographical position…

"The sides attach special significance to the strict observance of the UN Charter, the Helsinki Final Act, other fundamental international legal documents prohibiting aggression, the violation of borders, the seizure of other countries territories, all forms of the threat or use of force, and interference in other countries internal affairs on whatever pretext.

The "Brezhnev Doctrine"

Brezhnev, at a **July 1968** meeting with the Czech leadership, claimed a common Warsaw Pact responsibility for Czech defense. After the invasion the Soviets issued a proclamation known as the Brezhnev Doctrine that claimed Moscow's right to intervene when, in its opinion, socialism in any country of its commonwealth might be in danger (See Brezhnev in Pravda, 13 November 1968 above).

The following two documents were released at the end of the Cold War.

At a **24 July 1968** meeting in Budapest the Soviets told the Hungarians to begin preparations to invade Czechoslovakia. This was revealed in a memorandum of a conversation between Hungarian and Soviet military officials on the state of the final military planning for the invasion—code named Operation Danube.**

On **17 August 1968** at the conclusion of a three day meeting, the Soviet Politburo decided to intervene in Czechoslovakia with military force and unanimously approved a resolution to that end. The invasion took place 20/21 August 1968. The Resolution and attachments were released at the end of the Cold War.***

---

* See "Gorbachev Renounces Brezhnev Doctrine during Yugoslav Visit," FBIS Trends, 6 April 1988 pages 11-1

** In 1968 CIA analysts did not know about the July 1968 meeting. The information was not revealed until after the end of the Cold War, reported in Mastny and Byrne, A Cardboard Castle, xxxii.

*** For text of the memorandum, see Document No. 62 in The Prague Spring '68, National Security Archive Documents Reader, compiled and edited by Jaromir Navratil, The Prague Spring Foundation, (Budapest: Central European University Press, 1998). Ibid. For text of the resolution and accompanying documents, see Document No. 88

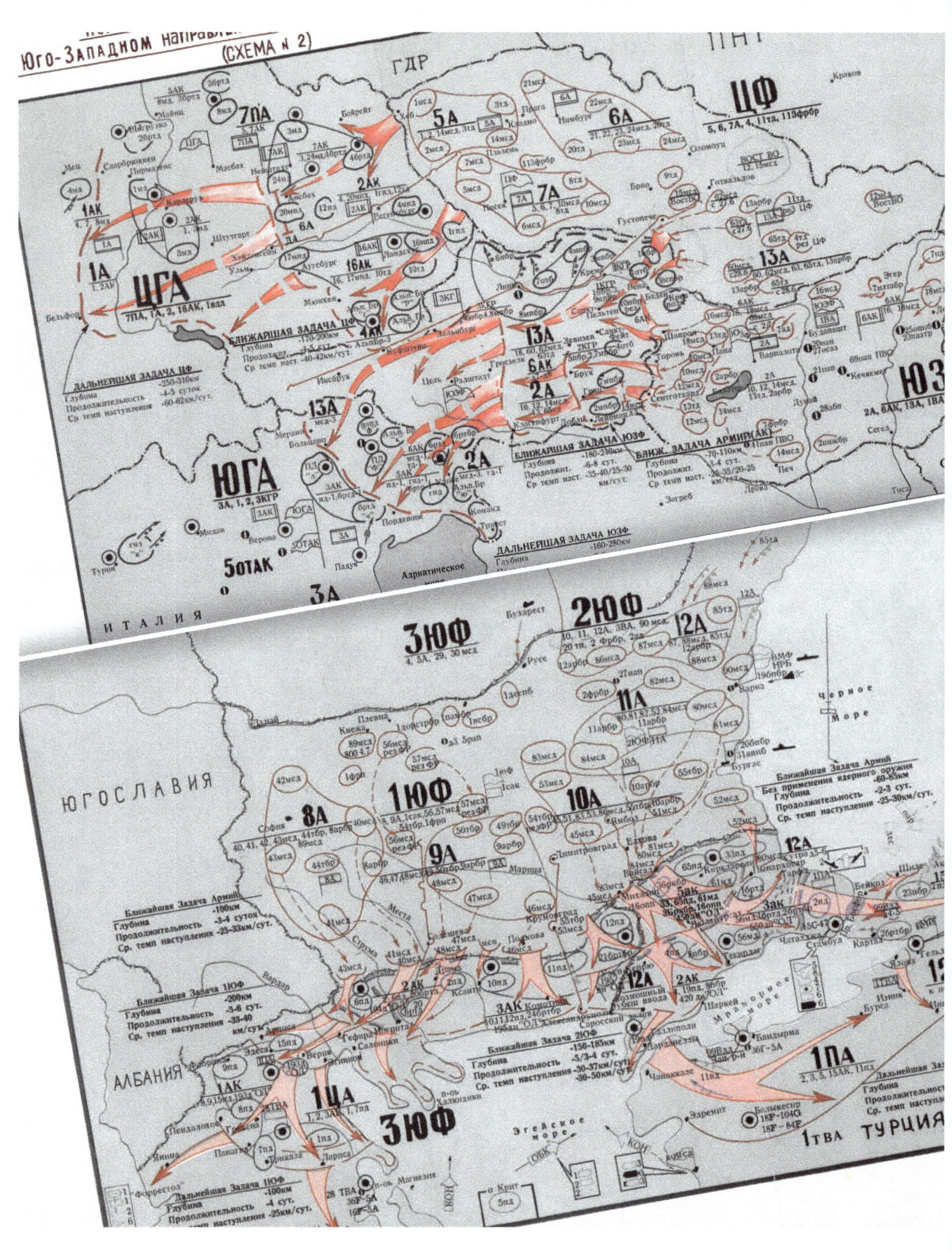

CHAPTER VII

Clandestine Reporting and the Analysis and Estimates of the Warsaw Pact (1970–1985)

Soviet-Warsaw Pact Developments and MBFR

Throughout the 1960s and into the 1980s, the decisiveness of strategic nuclear weapons was undisputed among Soviet military theorists. However, by the late 1960s and early 1970s discussions relating to the evolution of military doctrine elaborated on the increased probability that nuclear weapons would not be used in the initial or even later stages of a war with NATO in Europe. As new doctrine for conventional war evolved, so did demands for qualitative and quantitative changes for new weapons and forces in Europe. Nonetheless, the Soviets were constrained by the costs of building new divisions and armies opposite China, investing heavily in strategic weapons and the Navy, and trying to manage a floundering economy. In this context, even more than in the 1960s, the NSWP forces were an increasingly important component of the force opposite NATO in the central region of Europe. As the Soviets strove to meet all their perceived requirements, they demanded their reluctant allies participate more in the increased defense efforts. During this period the records of Soviet successes and failures prodding their Warsaw Pact allies to invest more in the military were often chronicled in clandestine services' disseminated intelligence information reports. Less precise reflections of the resulting strains appeared in various open sources.

The Soviets expanded and reequipped their ground forces to address the problems posed by a strategy to fight a war only with conventional weapons. They added tanks to the divisional structure, expanded artillery units and outfitted them with self-propelled weapons, and deployed new antiaircraft and antitank systems. They also expanded rear echelon support units. Finally, they developed new operational doctrine and established the Operational Maneuver Group as an important form of organization within plans for war in Europe. Clandestinely acquired writings exposed the thinking behind these changes and foretold much of what was to come.

By the 1970s, the Soviets also reacted to the potentially crippling impact of NATO airpower on Soviet ability to execute their war plan.[44] Soviet classified military theoretical journals and defector reports illustrated how the devastating effect of the Israeli Air Force in the 1967 Middle East War and the dominance of US tactical airpower in Vietnam seriously influenced Soviet military leaders. In response, the Soviets started developing new operational-strategic doctrine, strategy, and plans for massive air operations in Europe at the outset of hostilities. In the 1970s, they began to deploy more capable tactical aircraft that partially remedied the existing shortcomings in range, payload, and all-weather capability.

Managing the Warsaw Pact

The Warsaw Pact opened the 1980s with almost every member having "approved" virtually all of the Warsaw Treaty Statutes and having established new institutions to manage the alliance. Only Romania had not signed and ratified the statutes on 21 March 1978, and only the Statute on Unified Command for War Time had not been endorsed. The Pact, again minus Romania, finally approved, signed, and ratified that statute on 18 March 1980. Nonetheless, Soviet control of the alliance's forces continued to be a problem.

The authors of NIE 12/11-83 judged that, in Soviet eyes, the participation of East European forces would be crucial to success in a war with NATO in Europe. They noted the Soviets had taken a number of political and military actions to ensure cooperation but did not entirely control the effectiveness of these actions

---

[44] As reported in Chapters I and II, the Soviets, under Khrushchev, dramatically reduced the size of their tactical aviation forces in the late 1950s and early 1960s. At that time, Khrushchev and his military supporters expressed little interest in traditional massive land forces and associated aviation. They posited nuclear-armed missiles and long-range bombers as the decisive weapons of modern conflict. They reduced the light or tactical bomber force, for example, to about one-sixth of its former size. Other tactical aviation also suffered considerable decrements.

and remained concerned. The authors acknowledged they had no concrete evidence on the reliability of the East European forces. For the most part, they based their judgments on perceptions of the probable views of the NSWP countries, observations of precautionary actions by these countries, and estimates of probable behavior of NSWP forces under various circumstances.

Throughout this period the Soviets faced a persistent problem. They had to balance the policy of détente and the need for economic reform in the USSR and the NSWP member countries on the one hand against the political unrest in Eastern Europe and the need to maintain Warsaw Pact security on the other. The Soviets remained apprehensive about Romania's wayward course and its potential to contaminate the other members of the Warsaw Pact. Trouble was brewing again in Poland by the mid-1970s, and warming relations between East and West Germany posed potential problems for the Soviet Union. The Sino-Soviet dispute continued, and the Soviet puppet government in Afghanistan was failing. While the 1970s had begun with successful completion of the ABM Treaty and the SALT I agreement, the Soviet arms control agenda started to unravel a few years later. First, the United States cancelled the SALT II negotiations, and the policy of détente went belly up as the international community denounced Soviet military intervention in Afghanistan. Moreover, in 1979, the US administration, with concurrence of its NATO allies, moved to begin deployment of intermediate-range nuclear weapons in Europe by 1983 to deter or protect against potential Soviet nuclear attack.

Intelligence Sources and Analysis

In the years following the Soviet invasion of Czechoslovakia, the quantity and fullness of clandestinely obtained information about the Warsaw Pact military establishments increased at unprecedented rates. These new streams of reporting enabled analysts to develop assessments about the extent of cooperation among the Warsaw Pact members and the level of their future investment in military equipment. The Warsaw Pact war plans became clearer through the mosaic of evidence gleaned bit by bit from the wealth of classified documents clandestinely obtained from several of the Warsaw Pact members. Collection of technical intelligence blossomed as well, yielding a true bonanza for analysis and ultimately for all defense-related policymakers in the US government. CIA produced new assessments of Pact forces' readiness, logistical capabilities, mobilization and reinforcement capabilities, peacetime and wartime postures, and plans for wartime employment. The IC in general, especially DIA, also made good use of the mass of evidence from the clandestine efforts. Many of the more important CIA analytic publications are represented in the Catalogue of Documents.

The classified theoretical articles often betrayed misgivings—carefully—about the contemporary doctrine and strategy for Soviet forces. Other documents—field service manuals and General Staff Academy manuals and lectures—thoroughly described extant operational and tactical doctrine. Another group of documents describing and critiquing major exercises provided insight into the practical application of strategy and doctrine. The quantity and quality of all of these documents available from the end of the 1960s to 1985 provided the firmest basis yet for analysis and estimating Warsaw Pact military capabilities.

In the 1960s, much of the added impetus for producing more and better intelligence on the Warsaw Pact forces came from the Secretary of Defense, while in the early 1970s it came initially from National Security Advisor Henry Kissinger and his staff. In the 1960s the IC had reached a consensus about the size of the Warsaw Pact ground forces in terms of divisions and their equipment. There was not, however, enough known about above-division support, especially service support, to provide the basis for much more than gross extrapolations. In the 1970s the improved technical intelligence collection efforts yielded evidence of organizational and equipment changes in the deployed forces at all echelons as well as in production of new armaments. Those efforts and clandestine reporting of change in Soviet military thinking and of the demands being made by the Soviet leadership in Warsaw Pact councils provided a broader and firmer basis for assessing the rising conventional threat to NATO. Clandestine reporting provided a confident basis for new force readiness studies clearly more relevant than previously possible.

Through clandestine reporting, CIA military analysts were able to piece together the main elements of Soviet planning for a major air operation at the outset of hostilities with NATO. Classified military journals indicated Soviet military thinkers were on a quest for change in concepts for theater air operations as they sought to evaluate the full significance of the successes of the Israeli and US theater air operations. Later in the decade more evidence became available indicating which changes were actually incorporated in Soviet theater warfare doctrine for air operations. Previously, the Soviets had mainly viewed their tactical air forces as supporting the ground forces and delivering nuclear weapons. Consistent with long-held doctrinal views, the generally limited range and payloads of Soviet tactical aircraft as of 1970 restricted their usefulness to areas relatively close to the battlefront. Operations to the depth of the theater were the preserve of the missile forces and Long-Range Aviation, a strategic arm of the air forces analogous to the US Strategic Air Command (SAC).

Soviet classified writings reflected an evolution in military thinking that ended in a consensus about how to conduct initial air operations in the European theater, with the concept of a major theater-wide strategic air operation involving all theater aviation. The new strategy called for tactical aviation and strategic bombers to carry out missions massively at the outset of hostilities that were designed to achieve early air supremacy. The strategy emphasized the importance of such an operation in nonnuclear warfare when the Soviets saw their missiles, with limited payload and accuracy, to be of little value beyond the immediate battle area. Soviet aviation theorists also saw achievement of air supremacy in the initial stage of conflict as essential for the success of the ground operations.

CIA analysis based on Soviet classified writings and subsequent information described an intellectual ferment. The writings of air operations theorists suggested a certain sense of desperation inherent in the Soviet Air Operation Plan. In contrast, articles by Soviet ground forces officers reflected a confidence that NATO air forces would not make a critical difference in the outcome of a war in Europe. The latter view might have resulted from hubris or merely reflected the long-held primacy of ground forces doctrine in Soviet military thinking. For whatever reason, Soviet air forces, including Long-Range Aviation, were reorganized during the period 1978–81.

During approximately the same time period, the US national security establishment had added conventional arms control—Mutual and Balanced Force Reductions (MBFR)—to interests that required more of the IC than ever before. Policymakers demanded assessments of actual quantities of signature component parts of the forces, not extrapolated estimates. And they wanted more definitive assessments of the qualitative aspects of forces such as training, support, and materiel stocks. Interest in enhancing NATO defenses was also building. Some of the intelligence collection and analysis produced in support of the MBFR effort in effect overturned old assumptions about the Warsaw Pact forces, revealing opportunities for improving NATO defenses. Although there was political and military resistance among the Western allies to the changed appraisals of the balance between NATO and Warsaw Pact conventional forces, the IC's increasingly refined data and estimates during the 1970s provided the foundation for major changes in the defense posture of the United States and NATO allies. In particular, these new estimates formed a basis for influencing NATO efforts toward more secure defenses against the Warsaw Pact massed tank forces. The changes in NATO equipment, force posture and mobilization capabilities resonated with the Soviet military leadership and had repercussions for the future, as foretold in clandestinely obtained classified reporting.

In the course of preparing the basic data for MBFR negotiating positions, the NSC aggregated data on NATO from the Joint Chiefs of Staff (JCS) and on the Warsaw Pact forces from CIA and DIA and compared the two forces under several scenarios. These efforts exposed shortcomings in information the IC had not yet resolved. High-resolution satellite imagery was a great advancement, especially for revealing the extent of deployed forces and the technical characteristics (mensuration, etc.) of many weapons systems, but it did not provide the kind of evidence needed to support the more refined estimates required by the MBFR effort. New clandestine sources in the 1970s, by contrast, did yield a breakthrough in such evidence.

The wealth of material provided by clandestine sources, especially Colonel Kuklinski, provided other insights. It formed the basis of new judgments about the logistical capabilities to support the Pact's ambitious war plans. Shortfalls in training and readiness of Warsaw Pact forces became evident. The evidence also illustrated the differences in quality among the Warsaw Pact forces. The analysis of this evidence was reflected in numerous formal CIA publications and in unpublished replies to requests by the NSC staff, samples of which are reproduced in this study. That same evidence informed the production of other component agencies of the IC. Intelligence studies produced during the decade, based on the increasing quantity and quality of the collected evidence, reflected a growing analytic sophistication and a more comprehensive understanding of the Warsaw Pact forces building finally to the watershed 1979 National Intelligence Estimate: *Warsaw Pact Forces Opposite NATO* (NIE 11-14-79). The DO disseminated a virtual blizzard of reports during the period 1973–85, including more than 100 just on Warsaw Pact exercises. The reports also contained more than 60 documents, manuals, or lecture notes from the USSR General Staff Academy and other higher military academies. Summaries of these documents are located in the Catalogue of Documents.

Following is an excerpt from Chapter 4 of *How Much is Enough?* by Alain C. Enthoven.

© 1971, Alain C. Enthoven, K. Wayne Smith; 2005, Rand Corporation. Reprinted with permission. All rights reserved.

How Much Is Enough?
Shaping the Defense Program 1961–1969

ALAIN C. ENTHOVEN

K. WAYNE SMITH

For the complete chapter see How Much is Enough? contained in the attached DVD.

This is an excerpt from Chapter 4 of *How Much is Enough?* by Alain C. Enthoven.

For the complete chapter see *How Much is Enough?* contained in the attached DVD.

How Much is Enough? Chapter 4 – NATO Strategy and Forces, pg. 132–156

How Much is Enough? Chapter 4 – NATO Strategy and Forces, pg. 132–156

CIA ANALYSIS OF THE WARSAW PACT FORCES: THE IMPORTANCE OF CLANDESTINE REPORTING

How Much is Enough? Chapter 4 – NATO Strategy and Forces, pg. 132–156

CIA ANALYSIS OF THE WARSAW PACT FORCES: THE IMPORTANCE OF CLANDESTINE REPORTING

How Much is Enough? Chapter 4 – NATO Strategy and Forces, pg. 132–156

CIA ANALYSIS OF THE WARSAW PACT FORCES: THE IMPORTANCE OF CLANDESTINE REPORTING

How Much is Enough? Chapter 4 – NATO Strategy and Forces, pg. 132–156

How Much is Enough? Chapter 4 – NATO Strategy and Forces, pg. 132–156

How Much is Enough? Chapter 4 – NATO Strategy and Forces, pg. 132–156

How Much is Enough? Chapter 4 – NATO Strategy and Forces, pg. 132–156

How Much is Enough? Chapter 4 – NATO Strategy and Forces, pg. 132–156

How Much is Enough? Chapter 4 – NATO Strategy and Forces, pg. 132–156

How Much is Enough? Chapter 4 – NATO Strategy and Forces, pg. 132–156

CIA ANALYSIS OF THE WARSAW PACT FORCES : THE IMPORTANCE OF CLANDESTINE REPORTING

How Much is Enough? Chapter 4 – NATO Strategy and Forces, pg. 132–156

How Much is Enough? Chapter 4 – NATO Strategy and Forces, pg. 132–156

How Much is Enough? Chapter 4 – NATO Strategy and Forces, pg. 132–156

How Much is Enough? Chapter 4 — NATO Strategy and Forces, pg. 132–156

NATO pilot gets twice as many flying hours per month as the average Pact pilot. The average Pact aircraft spends more time out of commission per flying hour than the average NATO aircraft. Pilot training and aircraft maintenance are expensive, but they give us a more effective air force.

All these factors change the conclusions derived from a simple counting of aircraft. NATO air forces have much greater offensive power than the Pact. However, as with land forces, many of NATO's air advantages are only potential. They are in danger of being wasted because relatively inexpensive but critically important matters are being neglected. For example, the present vulnerability of our air bases could be reduced inexpensively. We badly need to build aircraft shelters. It makes little sense to refuse to invest $100,000 for a shelter to protect an aircraft costing between $2 and $8 million. We also need to establish better runway repair capabilities and to take other measures oriented toward providing more active and passive defense for our air bases. Otherwise, we are in danger of losing many aircraft in the first few days or hours of a war, as the Arabs did in 1967.

In summary, based on years of study, we believe that NATO's conventional forces are not smaller than those of the Pact and, therefore, that a strong conventional capability is feasible. This is not to say that NATO could defeat the Soviets or could unilaterally reduce its forces in safety. The balance is close—so close that even moderate changes can have a significant effect on the balance of military power. In addition, as we have pointed out repeatedly, there are a number of serious qualitative problems. We are not getting what we are paying for because we are not providing all the "horseshoe nails" needed to realize the full potential of NATO's existing conventional forces. The major missing nails include aircraft shelters, modern air ordnance, ground ammunition, and a larger allied mobilization capability. There is also considerable room for improvement in troop deployments, allied pilot training, manning levels, and training levels (resulting from short terms of service). By correcting these deficiencies, NATO could greatly increase the effectiveness of its conventional forces without big increases in costs. But to do so requires concentrating our efforts on solving the real problems of military readiness and effectiveness against realistic threats rather than spending so much time and effort devising ways of meeting an exaggerated threat.

This is an excerpt from Chapter 4 of *How Much is Enough?* by Alain C. Enthoven.
© 1971, Alain C. Enthoven, K. Wayne Smith; 2005, Rand Corporation.
Reprinted with permission. All rights reserved.

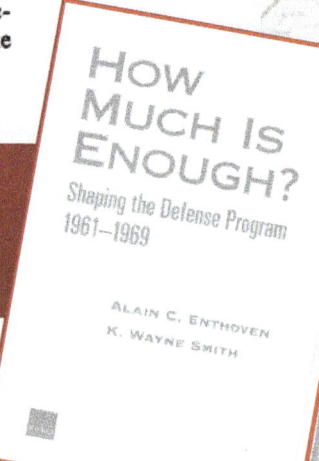

Acknowledgments

The CIA Historical Collections Division gratefully acknowledges the following for their courtesy and assistance in providing material for this collection:

> **National Security Agency** for their thorough review and assistance toward the declassification of documents for this study.

> **Defense Intelligence Agency** for the assistance of (DIA) officers who searched their archives for CIA reports not found in CIA archives.

> **National Geospatial Intelligence Agency** for their thorough review and assistance toward the declassification of documents for this study.

> **Alain C. Enthoven** for granting permission to include in this study, the chapter on "NATO Strategy and Forces" from his book – *How Much Is Enough: Shaping the Defense Program, 1961–1969*.

> We note the critical contribution to this project by the late **James (Les) Griggs (Colonel, US ARMY, Retired)** who brought his deep knowledge of the Warsaw Pact military to bear in evaluating and preparing for release the complex documents in this study.

> CIA's Imaging and Publishing Support (IPS) graphic artists John Bassett, Robert Karyshyn, and Mary Alexander.

Principal Contributors

A special thank you to those who searched for, located, reviewed and redacted more than 1,000 classified documents for the study:

John C. Guzzardo
James H. Noren
Anthony Williams
Terry A. Bender

and the two persons who initiated the project more than ten years ago:

Michael J. Sulick *former Deputy Director of Operations*
Herbert O. Briick *former Chief of the Information and Review Group, IMS*

Agency Disclaimer

All statements of facts, opinion, and analysis expressed in this booklet are those of the authors. They do not necessarily reflect official positions or views of the Central Intelligence Agency or any other US Government entity, past or present. Nothing in the contents should be construed as asserting or implying US Government endorsement of an articles statements or interpretations.

CIA ANALYSIS OF THE WARSAW PACT FORCES: THE IMPORTANCE OF CLANDESTINE REPORTING

Col Oleg Penkovskiy (top); Col Ryszard Kuklinski (middle right), Col Kuklinski assisting Minister of Defense of the Soviet Union signing the Wartime Statutes of the Warsaw Pact in 1979.(lower left); Maj (later Lt Col) Pyotr Popov (lower right)

CIA ANALYSIS OF THE WARSAW PACT FORCES: THE IMPORTANCE OF CLANDESTINE REPORTING

The Historical Collections Division (HCD) of CIA's Information Management Services is responsible for executing the Agency's Historical Review Program. This program seeks to identify and declassify collections of documents that detail the Agency's analysis and activities relating to historically significant topics and events. HCD's goals include increasing the usability and accessibility of historical collections. HCD also develops release events and partnerships to highlight each collection and make it available to the broadest audience possible.

The mission of HCD is to:

➢ Promote an accurate, objective understanding of the information and intelligence that has helped shape major US foreign policy decisions.

➢ Broaden access to lessons-learned, presenting historical material that gives greater understanding to the scope and context of past actions.

➢ Improve current decision-making and analysis by facilitating reflection on the impacts and effects arising from past foreign policy decisions.

➢ Showcase CIA's contributions to national security and provide the American public with valuable insight into the workings of its government.

➢ Demonstrate the CIA's commitment to the Open Government Initiative and its three core values: Transparency, Participation, and Collaboration.

The mission of the *National War College* is to educate future leaders of the Armed Forces, State Department, and other civilian agencies for high-level policy, command, and staff responsibilities by conducting a senior-level course of study in national security strategy.

The National War College (NWC) provides a single-phase Joint Professional Military Education (JPME) program for mid-career US military officers, civilian US government officials, and foreign military officers. We achieve our mission by offering a professional, rigorous, multi-disciplinary curriculum emphasizing active-learning and immersion in a joint environment. This joint experience is further enriched by the inclusion of interagency and multinational partners in all aspects of the program. The NWC program is accredited by the Middle States Commission on Higher Education, and qualified graduates are awarded a Masters of National Security Strategy.

DVD Contents

The Historical Collections Division and the Information Review Division of the Central Intelligence Agency's Information Management Services has reviewed, redacted, and released more than 1,000 documents highlighting CIA's analysis of the Warsaw Pact forces and the importance of clandestine reporting. Almost all of those documents were previously classified, some declassified earlier redacted with text now restored and released for this study. The accompanying DVD contains those documents as well as more than 500 previously released declassified documents, videos about the U-2 reconnaissance aircraft and CORONA satellite programs, and a gallery of related photos. The DVD also contains the essays in this booklet.

This DVD will work on most computers and the documents are in .PDF format.

The material is organized into the following categories:

→ The two essays printed in the booklet including the chapter 4 of Alain C. Enthoven's book *How Much Is Enough?* from which his essay is excerpted.;

→ **Document Catalogue and Collection**—Features intelligence assessments, National Intelligence Estimates, high-level memos, DCI talking points, and other reporting. To help put this material in perspective, we have also included related non-CIA documents from the Office of the Secretary of Defense, the National Security Council Staff and the Department of State and from the Wilson Center's Parallel History project replicating Soviet documents;

Previously released related declassified documents;

→ **Videos**—films showing some of the development of the U-2 reconnaissance aircraft and the CORONA reconnaissance satellite programs;

→ **Other Multimedia**—includes a gallery of photos including clandestine photos of Soviet maps showing variants of invasion plans used in a major Warsaw Pact exercise.

Warsaw Pact War Plan for Central Region of Europe

Summary
Intelligence Memorandum
Directorate of Intelligence
18 June 1968

The Warsaw Pact contingency plan for war with NATO in the Central Region of Europe – as revised by the Soviets in the early 1960s – assigns the initial offensive missions to the forces already deployed in East Germany, Czechoslovakia, and Poland. In addition, it gives both the Czechs and Poles command over their own national forces. After the initial objectives have been gained, Soviet forces in the western USSR would move quickly into the Central Region and take over the offensive against NATO.

Under the previous plan, the initial offensive would have been conducted mainly by Soviet forces, including those based in the western USSR, with the East European forces integrated into Soviet-led Fronts. This concept, to be effective, required a high level of combat readiness for the Soviet forces in the western USSR. The reduction of Soviet ground force strength in the early 1960's probably made this plan infeasible and stimulated concurrent improvements in the East European ground forces to permit them to assume greater responsibilities.

HISTORICAL COLLECTIONS

The Historical Review Program, part of the CIA Information Management Services, identifies, collects, and produces historically relevant collections of declassified documents.

These collections, centered on a theme or event, are joined with supporting analysis, essays, video, audio, and photographs, and showcased in a booklet plus DVD, and made available to historians, scholars, and the public.

All of our Historical Collections are available on the CIA Library Publication page located at https://www.cia.gov/library/publications/historical-collection-publications/ or contact us at HistoricalCollections@UCIA.gov.

www.ingramcontent.com/pod-product-compliance
Lightning Source LLC
Chambersburg PA
CBHW081926170426
43200CB00014B/2842